The Civil Rights Movement: A Very Short Introduction

VERY SHORT INTRODUCTIONS are for anyone wanting a stimulating and accessible way into a new subject. They are written by experts, and have been translated into more than 45 different languages.

The series began in 1995, and now covers a wide variety of topics in every discipline. The VSI library currently contains over 700 volumes—a Very Short Introduction to everything from Psychology and Philosophy of Science to American History and Relativity—and continues to grow in every subject area.

Very Short Introductions available now:

ABOLITIONISM Richard S. Newman
THE ABRAHAMIC RELIGIONS
   Charles L. Cohen
ACCOUNTING Christopher Nobes
ADDICTION Keith Humphreys
ADOLESCENCE Peter K. Smith
THEODOR W. ADORNO
   Andrew Bowie
ADVERTISING Winston Fletcher
AERIAL WARFARE Frank Ledwidge
AESTHETICS Bence Nanay
AFRICAN AMERICAN HISTORY
   Jonathan Scott Holloway
AFRICAN AMERICAN
   RELIGION Eddie S. Glaude Jr
AFRICAN HISTORY John Parker and
   Richard Rathbone
AFRICAN POLITICS Ian Taylor
AFRICAN RELIGIONS Jacob K. Olupona
AGEING Nancy A. Pachana
AGNOSTICISM Robin Le Poidevin
AGRICULTURE Paul Brassley and
   Richard Soffe
ALEXANDER THE GREAT
   Hugh Bowden
ALGEBRA Peter M. Higgins
AMERICAN BUSINESS HISTORY
   Walter A. Friedman
AMERICAN CULTURAL
   HISTORY Eric Avila
AMERICAN FOREIGN RELATIONS
   Andrew Preston
AMERICAN HISTORY Paul S. Boyer
AMERICAN IMMIGRATION
   David A. Gerber

AMERICAN INTELLECTUAL
   HISTORY Jennifer Ratner-Rosenhagen
THE AMERICAN JUDICIAL SYSTEM
   Charles L. Zelden
AMERICAN LEGAL HISTORY
   G. Edward White
AMERICAN MILITARY HISTORY
   Joseph T. Glatthaar
AMERICAN NAVAL HISTORY
   Craig L. Symonds
AMERICAN POETRY David Caplan
AMERICAN POLITICAL HISTORY
   Donald Critchlow
AMERICAN POLITICAL PARTIES
   AND ELECTIONS L. Sandy Maisel
AMERICAN POLITICS
   Richard M. Valelly
THE AMERICAN PRESIDENCY
   Charles O. Jones
THE AMERICAN REVOLUTION
   Robert J. Allison
AMERICAN SLAVERY
   Heather Andrea Williams
THE AMERICAN SOUTH
   Charles Reagan Wilson
THE AMERICAN WEST Stephen Aron
AMERICAN WOMEN'S HISTORY
   Susan Ware
AMPHIBIANS T. S. Kemp
ANAESTHESIA Aidan O'Donnell
ANALYTIC PHILOSOPHY
   Michael Beaney
ANARCHISM Alex Prichard
ANCIENT ASSYRIA Karen Radner
ANCIENT EGYPT Ian Shaw

For more information visit our website

www.oup.com/vsi/

Thomas C. Holt

THE CIVIL RIGHTS MOVEMENT

A Very Short Introduction

OXFORD
UNIVERSITY PRESS

Oxford University Press is a department of the University of Oxford.
It furthers the University's objective of excellence in research, scholarship,
and education by publishing worldwide. Oxford is a registered trade mark of
Oxford University Press in the UK and certain other countries.

Published in the United States of America by Oxford University Press
198 Madison Avenue, New York, NY 10016, United States of America.

Library of Congress Cataloging-in-Publication Data

Names: Holt, Thomas C. (Thomas Cleveland), 1942- author.
Title: The Civil rights movement : a very short introduction / Thomas C. Holt.
Other titles: Movement
Description: New York, NY : Oxford University Press, [2023] |
Series: Very short introductions | "Published in hardcover as The Movement: The
African American Struggle for Civil Rights (2021)." | Includes
bibliographical references and index.
Identifiers: LCCN 2022046991 (print) | LCCN 2022046992 (ebook) |
ISBN 9780190605421 (paperback) | ISBN 9780190605445 (epub)
Subjects: LCSH: African Americans—Civil rights—History—20th century. |
Civil rights movements—United States—History—20th century. |
African Americans—Social conditions—To 1964. | African Americans—
Social conditions—1964–1975. | Southern States—Race relations—History—
20th century. | United States—Race relations—History—20th century. |
United States—History—1953-1961. | United States—History—1961-1969.
Classification: LCC E185.61 .H755 2023 (print) | LCC E185.61 (ebook) |
DDC 2020035036—dc23/eng/20220930
LC record available at https://lccn.loc.gov/2022046991
LC ebook record available at https://lccn.loc.gov/2022046992

Printed and bound by
CPI Group (UK) Ltd, Croydon, CR0 4YY

Dedicated
to
Carrie Lee Price Fitzgerald (1878–1966),
who lived to see her world transformed
and
to all the Movement martyrs,
who did not

Contents

List of illustrations

Acknowledgments

It may seem odd that a very short book should have incurred such a long list of people to whom I am endebted, but most of these debts were acquired long before this project was even conceived. Some are owed to my maternal grandmother, Carrie, for the stories she shared during idle moments on our back porch about the history of the place we inhabited and in other more emotionally charged moments when she silently modeled for a preadolescent boy how one might negotiate its hostile terrain with dignity. Others are owed to my father, whose stories about how our family's history evolved in that hostile place and about the different worlds he had seen far beyond its confining and sometimes confounding boundaries somehow enabled me to think differently about my own place in the world. Growing up in a hostile world can make one self-destructive, but somehow these stories delegitimized its rule and suggested that building a very different world was possible.

All this prepared me to welcome others into my life whose influence on this book is even more direct. As I came of age, the Danville Movement brought Avon Rollins, Matthew Jones, James Forman, Dottie Miller, Bob Zellner, and Ivanhoe Donaldson to town, each of whom taught me much about the social movement they had witnessed taking shape and to which my peers and I were drawn. Lessons in nonviolent workshops with Ivanhoe (surely the most violent nonviolent person I have ever encountered), mass meetings with Avon, and jail cells shared with Matthew taught me much of what the Movement was about, what it aspired to be, and what it wasn't. As a student at Howard University during those years, I would learn more still, from a front-row seat to world-changing events and the bigger-than-life personalities among Howard's Nonviolent Action Group and the Student Nonviolent Coordinating Committee to which it was affiliated.

My more recent debts are owed to the students I have taught at the University of Michigan and the University of Chicago, some of whose works are cited in the endnotes to this book. Discussions with them in classes, during office hours, and in more casual conversations have provided alternative perspectives on social movements that have enriched my analysis. No doubt I got back more from them than I gave. Indeed, this book would not exist in its current form without the contributions to Movement historiography of Barbara Ransby, Laurie Beth Green, Janette Gayle, Quincy Mills, Traci L. Parker, and Elizabeth Todd-Breland. More recently, I owe a very special debt to Alexander Hofmann, whose diligent and careful collection of local census data provided the evidentiary basis for the principal themes organizing my analysis, which were otherwise based mostly on intuitions from personal experiences: that the roots and dynamics of the Movement in what I have called "New South cities" were very different from those in the rural Deep South, and that this matters both for how we recover this history and the uses we might make of it.

I am similarly grateful to my professional colleagues who have added so much to our knowledge of this history. Most are cited in the pages that follow, but three deserve special mention because not only did they alert me to stories about the Mississippi Movement that I did not know, but they also suggested ways of interpreting them I had not previously considered. For that I am especially grateful to Nan Woodruff, Charles Payne, and John Dittmer. I owe a debt as well to the Oxford University Press's anonymous readers, who alerted me to the necessity of at least commenting on issues I had neglected in my effort to keep this a truly "short history."

I also benefited from the enthusiasm and patience of my editor, Nancy Toff, and the efficient work of the editorial staff at Oxford University Press for nudging this book to a much delayed completion. As always Leora Auslander provided the right mixture of encouragement and a sharp editorial pen together with stimulating discussions about the international resonances of my analysis. Finally, I owe my greatest debt to Catherine Fitzgerald Holt for passing on my grandmother's story, which became the core theme of and inspiration for writing this book, and for the gift of her quiet joy upon hearing it retold.

Introduction: Carrie's rebellion

Carrie Lee Fitzgerald was sick with worry when she boarded the Trailways bus in Lynchburg headed to her home on the rural outskirts of Danville, Virginia, in January 1944. She had just visited her husband of forty-two years at the hospital for "coloreds," where he was being treated for kidney disease. She left fearing it might be the last time she saw him alive. And, indeed, he would die just a few days later. Perhaps her grief and state of mind explain her unexpected actions that day. Or perhaps it was the blatant contradiction between her treatment and the fact that at that very moment one of her three sons was serving with the American invasion army in Europe, while the husband of her youngest daughter—the one who accompanied her that day—was in the Pacific fighting on yet another front to "save the world for democracy." Or perhaps it was simply the accumulated insults over the course of her sixty-six years in a state that systematically demeaned and disrespected black life.

Whatever the cause, to her daughter's horror, she took a seat in the front of the bus—the section reserved for "whites." The driver noticed; he barked an order that she move to the back. Her reply cracked like a whip through the suddenly quiet bus, a tone all too familiar to her family and friends. She refused. Refused in no uncertain terms. The "cullid" seats, she pointed out, had been taken by the overflow of white college students who had filled the

1. The life of Carrie Fitzgerald, shown here with the author several months after challenging Virginia's segregation laws, bridged the struggles and aspirations of the generation born after the first Reconstruction and that of her grandchildren, who forged the second.

bus before she got on, so she was taking the first one freed by a departing passenger. Perhaps the driver found the prospect of wrestling an old lady out of her seat distasteful and the delay of waiting for the police inconvenient; in any event he decided to leave well enough alone, Virginia law and custom be damned. Thus Carrie rode the rest of the sixty miles to Danville undisturbed. Years later, family lore would celebrate her rebellion as "a Rosa Parks moment," an unsung rehearsal for the iconic beginning of the Civil Rights Movement ten years later.

Contrary to family lore, however, what is most notable about Carrie's rebellion is how representative it was of that moment in the history of black life in America, for there were certainly many similar rebellions, before and after. Indeed, just six months later, twenty-seven-year-old Irene Morgan, an employee of a defense contractor building fighter aircraft, would make a similar protest when she boarded a Greyhound bus at the Hayes Store stop near Gloucester, Virginia, for her trip home to Baltimore, Maryland. Unlike Carrie Fitzgerald, Irene Morgan was arrested, and her case subsequently attracted the attention of the nation and the legal team of the National Association for the Advancement of Colored People (NAACP), leading to a landmark decision two years later in which the US Supreme Court declared that because hers was a journey across state borders, the discrimination she suffered was an unconstitutional violation of her civil rights. Morgan's challenge to Virginia's Jim Crow laws may well have reflected her coming of age in a border state and the wartime activism of black Americans there, but each of these facts also reflects the changed environment across the nation for black aspirations for equal treatment and respect.

Fitzgerald's world in 1944 was very different from Morgan's, but it was also unlike the one she had been born into in 1878, just a year after the dreams of a democratically reconstructed South died in bloody violence and political betrayal. Not only did the war against Nazism offer promise of reviving that dream, but so had the material circumstances that made Carrie's resistance possible. Having left agricultural labor behind a decade earlier, her family was no longer dependent on the whims of a plantation boss for either subsistence or shelter. The dependents' allowance the army paid to her youngest daughter had enabled the purchase of the two-story log cabin that the family had previously rented. So there would be no landlord demanding an explanation for her actions on the bus that day. Nor was there anyone to threaten the jobs of her grown children, for by then those not in military service were employed in the southern or northern urban labor markets that had expanded to satisfy wartime demand, setting a pattern that would consolidate the massive demographic transformation that reshaped black life by the second half of the twentieth century.

Thus does Carrie Fitzgerald's story—arguably more than Irene Morgan's—reflect the crucial changes of the decades preceding the advent of the Civil Rights Movement. Nonetheless, like many similar events, recorded or lost to history, Carrie's individual and momentary challenge to the South's Jim Crow regime should not be conflated with later events as simply an early episode in what some have called "the long civil rights movement." Rather it must be seen as at best a prelude to that movement, one emblematic of the ongoing historical transformations that made a broader rebellion possible ten years later. The challenges to the Jim Crow order between 1955 and 1965 were clearly rooted in the generations of resistance that came before, and they cannot be understood without that prior history, but one must be clear that Carrie Fitzgerald's rebellion was *not yet* part of a mass social movement. In contrast to protests a decade later, there would be no community mobilization to build on her individual protest, nor much immediate change in her own disposition toward the oppression she had briefly challenged. She would quietly return to her usual routines, minding her garden and grandchildren. What many scholars have called the "classic" Civil Rights Movement, which spanned the decade between 1955 and 1965, is best understood, then, as a unique moment in the long history of African American resistance and struggle against racist oppression, a moment that included many of the elements missing from Carrie's story. We must recognize as well, however, that that later moment was rooted in and built on the social, economic, and geopolitical transformations that made Carrie's actions possible and that also shaped the conditions of possibility for the coming storm. In Carrie's story, then, we find the seeds of the larger story that would unfold for her children and grandchildren over the decades to come, all of whom would come of age in a different world than the one she had known.

Carrie's story also exposes some of the popular misconceptions about the character of, and the social forces driving, the movement that came later. The Civil Rights Movement has become a well-narrated era of recent American history. Its images re-broadcast every January and February in tandem with celebrations of Martin Luther King Jr.'s birthday and Black History Month have far too often been reduced to select soundbites of King's eloquence. Even when supplemented with the image of Rosa Parks's iconic sit-in on that Montgomery bus, the Movement is most often represented as the individual or collective acts of heroic and charismatic male leaders. Much like Carrie's lone act of rebellion, however, a deeper examination of the Movement reveals a resistance less driven by heroic male leaders showing the way than simply the accumulated grievances of ordinary citizens—most often women like Carrie Fitzgerald, Irene Morgan, and Rosa Parks—newly conscious of the means and possibility to act. Understanding both the limitations and the achievements of the Civil Rights Movement, therefore, requires that we recover the features, the historical conjuncture, that made it truly a social movement—collective, sustained, and world-changing.

The most active participants in the social movement that gripped the country for roughly a decade during the mid-twentieth century were very cognizant of its distinctive qualities: collective action, sustained commitment, and the determination to achieve fundamental changes in the social order and in the power relations that sustained it. Those activists summarized that engagement in two words, "The Movement." Occurring in different places, under different organizational auspices, with sometimes different specific objectives, its singular character— signaled textually by the definite article and the capital letters— was that ordinary people were *moving* in unison to achieve what they hoped would be revolutionary change. Certainly, there was a touch of arrogance and demonstrable error in some of the younger activists' assumptions that they were the very first to challenge and resist the absurdities and brutalities of America's racial order. On that point Carrie Fitzgerald and Irene Morgan could have set them straight. Their intuitive sense that they were coming of age at a distinctive moment in the long history of that freedom struggle was correct, however. Let us hope that a better understanding of the conditions of possibility shaping that struggle will be of use to the continuing struggle for social justice and human dignity.

Chapter 1
Before Montgomery

Many of the historical transformations that would reshape the everyday lives and consciousness of people like Carrie Fitzgerald and Irene Morgan had been set in motion by the First World War. The vast war-induced migration out of the South that began in 1916 would eventually break the stranglehold of the southern plantation regime on black life, bringing in its wake not only a fundamental reshuffling of the nation's racial geography but also a reconfigured social and political terrain. On this new ground the efficacy of African Americans' century-long struggle for human rights would be transformed, and neither the South nor the nation would be the same thereafter.

A legacy of protest

It is perhaps ironic that on April 2, 1917, Woodrow Wilson, the president who had brought the southern racial order to the nation's capital, also set the table for challenges to that regime when he asked Congress to declare war on Germany, in order, he assured the nation, for the world to "be made safe for democracy." The war that followed not only accelerated changes in the nation's racial demography but also quickened African Americans' demands for equality. On July 28, 1917, less than four months after Congress's declaration of war, black Americans marched down New York's Fifth Avenue in a silent protest, demanding democracy at home. They were responding both to a bloody race riot in East St. Louis three weeks earlier and to the wave of racial violence then ravaging black communities more generally. Marching from Fifty-Seventh to Twenty-Fourth Street to the funereal cadence of muffled drums, these ten thousand men, women, and children created a striking visual spectacle of their rightful claims on the nation. The children made up the front ranks of the march, while women dressed in white and men in black followed, their dignity and decorum underscoring claims to respect and national belonging. A few of the men wore their army uniforms, driving home a central theme etched on one of the signs they carried: "We have fought for the liberty of white Americans in six wars; our reward is East St. Louis."

2. In July 1917 ten thousand African Americans marched through midtown Manhattan in a silent parade protesting antiblack violence in East St. Louis, Missouri.

Although the timing and context of the Easter Sunday demonstration were exceptional, its message and tactics echoed earlier protests and anticipated others to follow. Indeed, the marchers exploited tactics then decades old, beginning in the contentious years preceding the Civil War and continuing well into the first decade of the twentieth century. For more than half a century, black Americans had turned to consumer boycotts and militant sit-ins to protest discriminatory treatment in public places. In 1854, when Elizabeth Jennings, a teacher and church organist, was ejected from New York's Third Avenue Railway, black activists in that city sprang into action, organizing protests and lodging a legal challenge. Securing the services of future president Chester Arthur's law firm, they exploited legal precedent holding that common carriers, having been granted access to the public way, were obligated to serve the *entire* public without discrimination, except in cases in which the "unfitness" of a passenger was clear, such as disease, unruly behavior, or unsavory appearance. None of these defects applied to Elizabeth Jennings.

Jennings's victory reflected the growing militancy of northern free blacks of that era, many of whom joined and recast the abolitionists' campaign against slavery to embrace agitation against racial discrimination as well. The increased use of horse-drawn streetcars in northern antebellum cities coincided with the rapid growth of a large and increasingly militant free black population, a conjuncture especially evident in Philadelphia, which had not only the largest free black population in antebellum North America but also nineteen streetcar and suburban rail lines. All of that city's streetcars either refused service to black passengers outright or subjected them to discrimination, often by forcing them to ride on outside platforms. The Negro Convention Movement, meeting there in the very same year as the Jennings protest, voiced its support for a petition campaign that William Still—famous later as a "conductor" for the Underground Railroad—had organized to protest racial discrimination on its streetcars.

3. Elizabeth Jennings, a church organist in New York City, sued a streetcar company in 1854 after she was denied service on her way to church on July 16 that year.

Most antebellum protests had taken the form of petitions and lawsuits, like those Still and Jennings initiated, but wartime protests a decade later turned to direct action as well. In northern cities during the war and in southern cities afterward, angry blacks boarded horse-drawn cars reserved for whites and relinquished their seats only after pitched battles with conductors or police. Prefiguring tactics deployed in the 1917 East St. Louis protest, the demonstrators often highlighted the blatant contradiction between black patriotism in war and the denial of equal rights in peace by having black soldiers and veterans lead the way, effectively staking their claims to the "new birth of freedom" Lincoln had recently proclaimed as the war's raison d'être. Their protests often drew attention to spectacular scenes of wounded black Union soldiers being ejected from streetcars, some of which appeared in the British press precisely at the moment when the possibility that Great Britain might openly support the Confederacy seemed imminent. Across the nation, black veterans' presence was emblematic of the connection demonstrators sought to draw between their access to public space and their claim to equal citizenship, a claim that their soldiers' sacrifice marked "paid in full."

Not only did these earlier incidents reveal the historical lineage of African Americans' struggle to gain recognition of their fundamental human rights and dignity, but they also rehearsed the basic strategies and tactics that later protests would adopt as well—sit-ins, boycotts, and mass street demonstrations—each capable of creating a veritable theater exposing grievances and injuries, and each aimed at rallying a persuadable public to demand justice, or failing that creating public disorder sufficient to force either the private companies or the state to act.

Perhaps the most striking fact about these earlier protests, in contrast with most later ones, was that they were successful. The national climate immediately following the Civil War often proved receptive to claims grounded in obvious patriotic sacrifices. A protest launched in Louisville, Kentucky, on October 30, 1870, reflects the changed political and legal climate after the war. With three hundred of their fellow parishioners looking on, Robert and Samuel Fox and their business partner, Horace Pearce, left Sunday services at Quinn Chapel and took seats on the horse-drawn trolley that passed their church in what was clearly a prearranged challenge to the legality of the Central Passenger Railroad Company's recently imposed segregation policy. They were attacked and dragged into the street before being arrested by police. Their actions triggered mass protests—"ride-ins"—during which black passengers sometimes seized the cars and drove themselves to their destinations. Eventually, the mayor brokered a settlement with the streetcar company. Meanwhile, their legal case had been moved from state to federal jurisdiction, where on May 11, 1871, the Fox brothers prevailed.

The Fox brothers' victory is noteworthy for its place and timing—a southern state during the early days of Reconstruction—but it was one among many instances when black people boarded streetcars and refused to move until ejected by drivers or police. Both southern and northern cities witnessed violent conflicts similar to those in Louisville, with black crowds gathering to support the "ride-in," while white mobs jeered and threw stones. This earlier era of black militancy culminated with the passage of a national Civil Rights Act in 1875, which outlawed discrimination on all public conveyances as well as in restaurants, theaters, and other facilities open to the general public.

For eight years the issue of black access to public spaces appeared to be settled law, notwithstanding unreliable enforcement. Lawsuits challenging the latter led in 1883 to the adjudication of a cohort of cases before the US Supreme Court, which declared the 1875 Civil Rights Act unconstitutional on the grounds that the federal government could punish the discriminatory acts only of states, not of private persons. Thirteen years later, the Court went farther, declaring in *Plessy v. Ferguson* in 1896 that the racial discrimination required by a state law in Louisiana was also valid, because "equal but separate" facilities had been provided. Although the *Plessy v. Ferguson* case referenced segregated train service specifically, the Court's "equal but separate" edict was soon applied to all aspects of interracial contact. In time, the word order would be reversed to "separate but equal," silently confirming the fact that the defense of segregation was its principal goal all along.

As states rushed to segregate transportation facilities in *Plessy*'s aftermath, however, a new series of black protests erupted. With the law and national political climate turned decisively against legal remedies for racial discrimination, black Americans turned once again to the boycott as the weapon of choice to protest the loss of legal protection of their civil rights. In the closest historical parallel to the direct-action movements of the 1950s, streetcar boycotts were launched in twenty-five cities in the Upper South between 1900 and 1906. Unlike the protests of the Civil War and Reconstruction eras, however, those of the early twentieth century did not succeed.

By the turn of the century, the nation's attitude toward racial equality had radically changed. The language of the majority opinion in the Supreme Court's 1883 Civil Rights Cases had effectively declared that black citizens were entitled to "no special protections" of their civil status, a judgment reconfirmed even more explicitly in the Court's rejection later of Homer Plessy's plea for equal justice. Meanwhile, the Republican Party adopted a southern electoral strategy designed to appeal to whites at the expense of blacks, giving a green light to southern legislatures to legislate in ways that they had not dared earlier because they feared intervention by federal legislative or judicial authorities. Over the next three decades, with that fear mooted, southern states deployed state power *to require* segregation, adopting overt measures to regulate blacks' presence in all kinds of public spaces while driving them from the ballot box as well. Thereafter black voter disfranchisement, previously achieved through subterfuge, trickery, and violence, was enshrined in explicit statutes and state constitutional provisions. These initiatives also created the atmosphere for a broader white backlash against blacks' literal presence in public spaces as well as curtailing their political and economic initiatives. Consequently, a wave of violence swept the South during the 1890s and early 1900s, including spectacular public lynchings and bloody urban riots in northern as well as southern cities, developments that triggered a steady out-migration to the North and West. This migration would accelerate tenfold a decade later.

The rise of the NAACP

By the second decade of the twentieth century, the Jim Crow regime was thoroughly entrenched in the South and had begun to emerge as customary practice in many parts of the North as well, notwithstanding the fact that in 1880s and 1890s some northern states had passed civil rights laws barring such practices. In fact, before the *Plessy* decision, the practice of separating blacks from whites in public spaces had been inconsistent and largely governed by private decisions in much of the South as well as the North. In *Plessy*'s aftermath, however, segregation became rigid and mandated by state law throughout the South. Thus stigmatized in public and deprived of voting rights, black Americans were officially marked by law as inferiors in the social order. Their degraded social and political status also rendered them vulnerable to the rising tide of racial violence sweeping through northern as well as southern cities over the decade that followed. Just two years after *Plessy*, for example, a sustained campaign in the state's press to vilify black men as rapacious beasts undeserving of voting rights paved the way to murderous rioting in Wilmington, North Carolina. In New Orleans and New York City in 1900 and Atlanta in 1906, rioting took on a pogrom-like aspect: no longer simply attacks on individuals but efforts to drive blacks from the city altogether by burning their homes and businesses and destroying their communities.

The most historically significant of these eruptions occurred
in 1908 in Springfield, Illinois. Violence resembling
contemporaneous attacks on Eastern European Jews in the
city most closely identified with Abraham Lincoln, the great
emancipator, shocked the nation, underscoring for many that
racial injustice was now clearly a national problem that had to
be addressed. Oswald Garrison Villard, scion of a venerable
abolitionist family and editor of the *New York Evening Post*,
initiated a call for a national, biracial conference to meet in New
York City in 1909 for the purpose of organizing a more effective
resistance, both to the violence and to the broader deprivation of
blacks' civil rights. The signal result of the conference was the
formation of the National Association for the Advancement of
Colored People (NAACP), which would become the most enduring
and often the central organization in the twentieth-century civil
rights struggle.

Of the sixty signatories endorsing Villard's "Call," however, only
seven were African American. Since even fewer of those were in a
position to work full time for the new organization, prominent
white northern antiracist activists filled the organization's
principal offices initially. W. E. B. Du Bois, editor of the NAACP's
magazine, *The Crisis*, was for many years the only African
American on staff. Perhaps reflecting the talents and orientation
of a staff made up mainly of lawyers and publicists, the initial
agenda and program of the organization focused heavily on legal
action and publicizing racial atrocities through its magazine. The
NAACP filed suits to outlaw peonage and residential segregation
and launched a decades-long lobbying campaign to secure federal
antilynching legislation.

Notwithstanding its initial scarcity of black officers, the NAACP
epitomized the institutional and human link between the earlier
black protest tradition and the movement that would emerge
later. Many of the men and women—black and white—answering
Villard's call had been shaped by, or were, like him, legatees of

nineteenth-century movements to abolish slavery and to craft a newly reconstructed nation afterward. Most had been active already in mounting the resistance to the recent onslaught of racist violence. Equally important was the organization's institutional legacy. It built on the earlier work and drew from the membership of diverse black protest organizations founded over the previous decade: the National Association of Colored Women's Clubs formed in 1896, the National Afro-American Council in 1898, and the Niagara Movement in 1905.

For more than four decades, from 1910 to 1954, the NAACP probed and finally broke through the legal weaknesses of the Jim Crow regime, convincing a unanimous US Supreme Court to outlaw segregation in public schools in *Brown v. Board of Education of Topeka.* During the years leading up to that decision, the organization had provided the essential platform for a broad assault on racial injustice, nurturing in the process a new generation of black litigators. The NAACP matured within the context of an increasingly urbanized and educated black population, anchored by relatively autonomous institutional foundations.

Indeed, from its beginnings, the most striking feature of the NAACP was the fact that it was headquartered in New York City and that its largest and most active chapters were in cities, southern as well as northern. It was in cities that the organization would find the financial support and legal talent to pursue its goals, especially among a new generation of African Americans. Over time, by publicizing black social and cultural achievements, Du Bois's *Crisis* attracted greater and broader public support for the organization, while at the same time calling into being a politically self-conscious black urban elite. By 1920, 85 percent of the organization's financial support came from black people, an initial surge in membership and funds that almost certainly reflected a northern urban population swollen by the in-migration of 1.5 million southern blacks during the First World War and the postwar decade.

NAACP chapters were established in rural areas as well, but the explosive wartime growth of the black population in southern cities was the crucial anchor of that region's most important branches. Even before the war, booming southern cities like Atlanta had developed the critical infrastructure of educational, financial, and legal talent that could facilitate and sustain protest initiatives. Among the founding members of the Atlanta branch, for example, were John Hope, the president of Atlanta University; Benjamin J. Davis, editor of the *Atlanta Independent*; A. D. Williams, pastor of the Ebenezer Baptist Church (a predecessor of Martin Luther King Sr.); and Harry Pace, an executive at the Standard Life Insurance Company. Indeed, perhaps no one better exemplifies the fortuitous emergence of this newly minted, southern, urban black upper-middle-class elite than Austin Thomas ("A. T.") Walden. Born in Fort Valley, Georgia, in 1885, Walden had witnessed a lynching in his youth before escaping the rural South to study with Du Bois at Atlanta University and then at the University of Michigan Law School. After serving as an officer with the 365th Infantry in France during World War I, he returned to begin a law practice in Macon before moving to Atlanta. Although his practice in Atlanta was built mainly on service to the city's black business elite, Walden emerged as a legal activist as well, albeit with a preference for approaches that were pragmatic and shrewd rather than confrontational. Nonetheless, as the principal organizer of Atlanta's Gate City Bar Association, a member of the civil rights committee of the black National Bar Association, and a close confidant of Thurgood Marshall, Walden would be a key figure in civil rights litigation for half a century.

A northern contemporary of Walden's was Charles Hamilton Houston. Born and raised in Washington, DC's middle class, his father a lawyer and his mother a schoolteacher, Houston took an approach to civil rights litigation that contrasted sharply with Walden's. Houston graduated from the capital's renowned M Street High School (Dunbar High after 1916), and like many others among that school's distinguished graduates, he continued his education at Amherst College and Harvard Law School, where he was elected to the *Law Review* and mentored in the avant-garde of legal realism by Felix Frankfurter. On the other hand, a sense of his youthful politics is suggested by his membership in the Harvard Negro Club, which at his invitation hosted Marcus Garvey for lunch. That encounter reflects something of the fluidity of black political consciousness in an era when, as Langston Hughes put it, "blackness was in vogue." As the principal organizer of the largest mass movement to date, Garvey's black nationalist agenda posed a powerful challenge to the NAACP's integrationist commitments at the time, ones Houston would soon dedicate himself to achieving.

Like Walden, Houston had served as an officer during the war, but he eventually chose a career teaching the law rather than follow his father into private practice. A decade later, as a professor at Howard University School of Law, Houston would refine and lead the NAACP's legal assault on segregation in America's public schools. Notwithstanding their differences in regional origin and temperament, therefore, Walden and Houston exemplified the vanguard of professional activists who emerged during the interwar period.

At that time they were also part of the largest generational cohort of college-educated men and women in African American history, many of whom had also received graduate training at the nation's most elite schools. Some of the men were radicalized politically by their war experiences, while the women as well as the men were drawn to the political activism that diverse and dynamic urban centers encouraged and supported during the interwar period. These men and women would go on to fill key leadership roles during the NAACP's second and third decades, challenging and extending the organization's mission and efficiency. Collectively they would shape the political and conceptual terrain for the movement that emerged in the 1950s and 1960s.

Despite the fact that many of the interwar generation were groomed and credentialed in predominantly white, elite universities, however, America was still thoroughly segregated, so these men and women pursued their professional careers in black colleges and universities and civic organizations. Indeed, one of the striking (and telling) ironies of a movement that sought to dismantle segregated institutions was that it was nurtured in predominantly black institutions. Barred from membership in the American Bar Association, black lawyers formed a separate National Bar Association in 1925 and they practiced and perfected their skills in segregated intellectual communities, like Howard University. Thus, it was in Howard's moot courtroom that the NAACP's challenge to segregated public education would be planned and tested.

On the other hand, the emergence of potential allies among their white contemporaries proved crucial to their success, as well. Funding from Charles Garland's American Fund for Public Service underwrote the initial planning and litigation that would eventually lead to the *Brown* decision, for example. Meanwhile, the rise of a more radical, antiracist labor movement provided both institutional support and foot soldiers for many black initiatives. Thus many of the key civil rights organizers of the 1950s and 1960s received their training in the Highlander Folk School, which had been established in 1932 to train white labor organizers before opening its residency program to blacks in 1944.

War, New Deal, and new antiracist strategies

The political and social opening for a sustained, ultimately successful attack on the Jim Crow regime emerged with the Great Depression of the 1930s and the world's second war for democracy in the 1940s. The first event produced a political realignment that diminished the white South's political stranglehold on the nation's capacity to respond to forces unleashed by the First World War; the second reframed the international context for pursuing racial justice initiatives nationally. The new environment also recast black Americans' sense of possibility, prompting a debate over the most effective tactics and strategies for achieving equal justice.

World depression delegitimized conventional thinking about the capitalist economy as a basis for democratic governance, and this strongly influenced the emerging interwar generation of black as well as white progressives. Even the sixty-four-year-old W. E. B. Du Bois, finding strong reasons to question the NAACP's unwavering commitment to a legal strategy and integrationist goals, decided to open a debate on these issues in the pages of the *Crisis* during the spring of 1932. In that debate Du Bois's embrace of socialist ideas aligned him with many of the younger generation of black activists. Far more controversial, however, was his conclusion that the exclusive commitment to integration was wrongheaded and that separatist black institutions offered a more promising basis for success in the long-term struggle for equal rights. Having effectively declared no confidence in the organization's philosophy and being irreconcilably at odds with the new leadership team of Walter White and Roy Wilkins, Du Bois would resign from the NAACP in June 1934.

In the meantime, however, the issues Du Bois had raised were clearly resonant with ongoing debates among intellectuals sparked by the national economic crisis. The question of the NAACP's strategic direction was aired during a retreat in Amenia, New York, in August 1933, after which the organization began taking tentative steps to form alliances with the rising labor movement and worked with reform-oriented officials in Franklin D. Roosevelt's New Deal administration. Meanwhile, the weakening of African American support for the Republican Party became evident in the 1934 midterm elections, when black voters in several northern cities defected. This initial break with the Republicans would become a landslide in the next presidential contest, making northern blacks a growing and potentially decisive constituency within the Democratic Party and thus reshaping the national political landscape. The Roosevelt administration's economic policies were clearly of potential benefit to an impoverished black population, despite the many discriminatory provisions embedded in New Deal programs by a still potent southern congressional delegation. It also helped that there were a number of well-placed white progressive administrators who offered real as well as symbolic support for the black agenda. A number of black intellectuals also served in influential positions in New Deal agencies; some of them had been among the conferees at Amenia. Moreover, discriminatory programs like the National Recovery Administration labor codes would emerge as targets for effective protest by those outside government.

Arguably, however, the New Deal's impact on the federal judiciary had a far deeper and more enduring impact in advancing black civil rights than its civil servants did. For the next three decades, Roosevelt's appointees to the Supreme Court made it increasingly receptive to the strategy Houston and Marshall pursued: to chip away at the separate but equal principle that the *Plessy* decision had enshrined in American law. Beginning with Lloyd Gaines's suit to gain admission to the University of Missouri Law School in 1938 and coming to fruition with Linda Brown's successful challenge to the South's segregated grade schools in 1954, their legal strategy probed, case by case, the inherent logical weaknesses of the separate but equal doctrine, which was quite simply that southern schools were not by any objective measure equal and that those states had neither the political will nor financial capacity to make them so. It could be easily demonstrated that from grade school through college, southern schools vastly shortchanged blacks. Finally, the NAACP's argument in 1954 supporting Linda Brown's suit against the Topeka school board convinced the Court that these inequities were inherent to a separation policy intended to stigmatize black citizens.

Arguably, the eventual success of the NAACP's legal assault against the South's racial regime owed at least as much to the broader political and social forces unleashed a decade earlier by the New Deal's responses to the Depression and later reinforced by a second world war as to the legal skills of its lawyers. First, the economic mobilization that began even before America's entry into World War II renewed black migration to northern and southern cities, thus further shifting the nation's overall racial demography. Second, roughly a million black men and women served in the armed forces, which dramatically reshaped blacks' consciousness and sense of entitlement. Each of these provided the context for black labor leader A. Philip Randolph's threat to mobilize an unprecedented march on Washington to demand equal access to both government and federally financed private-sector jobs in defense industries, a demand to which Roosevelt reluctantly acceded. Randolph's Brotherhood of Sleeping Car Porters—another Jim Crow institution that ironically anchored black resistance to segregation—would remain an important force in the struggle for racial justice for at least two more decades.

A new day coming: The turning point

By 1944, the war was at a turning point; with the Normandy invasion that summer, final victory against the Nazis seemed imminent. For many, a victory over Jim Crow also seemed within reach. Indeed, surveying these recent developments at the NAACP's convention in Chicago that year, Thurgood Marshall predicted that 1944 would be "a beachhead" in the long struggle against racism. His military metaphor might well have referenced ideological developments like the long-awaited publication that January of Gunnar Myrdal's *An American Dilemma*, which argued that the long-discussed "Negro Problem" was in fact a moral dilemma of white Americans, or alternatively, perhaps, the US Supreme Court's *Smith v. Allwright* decision in April outlawing the white primary, which sparked voter registration campaigns in the Deep South and a dramatic expansion of black voter enrollments over the next eight years. Marshall's optimism would likely have been confirmed, moreover, had he known that just days later a young black female defense worker, Irene Morgan, would challenge segregated seating on a Greyhound bus, an act that he would seize on later to win a court decision establishing the legal grounds for direct-action campaigns over the next decade, including the Montgomery bus boycott.

Later that year as well, the NAACP joined with radical labor and other progressive organizations to mount a drive that registered an estimated 600,000 black voters across the South by 1946—roughly 400,000 more than were recorded in 1940. Although there were no breakthroughs achieved with respect to changing the balance of power in the region as a whole, black voters did begin to have an impact on some local and congressional elections. Across the South, the early postwar years saw dramatic expansions of the black voter pool in Deep South states. Black voter registration in Georgia, for example, reached 135,000 in 1946, which was almost seven times the 20,000 on the rolls two years earlier. Despite ups and downs over the rest of the decade, the 3 percent of southern blacks registered in 1940 would grow to 20 percent by 1952.

Given this progress, Marshall's remarks no doubt also anticipated favorable prospects for black political fortunes at the Democratic convention scheduled to convene in Chicago just five days after he spoke. It turned out that events at the convention would challenge his assumptions about blacks' continued progress, however. In hindsight the convention appears instead to have been the opening round of a backlash against the ongoing struggle to redefine the agenda of the Democratic Party and the legacy of New Deal liberalism, all to the detriment of black Americans' welfare. For example, the challenge by a biracial group of progressive delegates from South Carolina to the seating of the all-white state delegation was defeated, the first of several indicators that the tide was turning against the party's antiracist potential. The fact that southern oligarchies had regained the upper hand in party councils was further underscored by FDR's acquiescence to the unceremonious dumping of Henry Wallace, his liberal vice-president. Wallace was replaced by a relatively obscure senator from Missouri, Harry Truman, a move widely seen as a victory for the southern white wing of the party.

Black Americans hardly knew what to expect when Truman became president after Roosevelt's sudden death nine months later. Not unlike Roosevelt, Truman would sound an uncertain trumpet with respect to the struggle for equal rights. His anti-Communist foreign policy aggravated the conservative-versus-progressive split within the party, eventually leading to the alienation and even prosecution of prominent black leftists like Du Bois and Paul Robeson. On the other hand, the party's sharp losses in the 1946 midterm elections, which were attributable in part to reduced support by northern blacks, led the president to reverse course and attempt to shore up his liberal base. Thus, a month after the 1946 midterms Truman established the President's Committee on Civil Rights, the first of many biracial bodies constituted to investigate racist practices. A year later the committee recommended ending the poll tax and making permanent and extending the mandate of the Fair Employment Practices Commission (FEPC) that FDR had established in 1941.

Although Truman eventually forwarded the Committee on Civil Rights' report to Congress for legislative action, his initial commitments to civil rights had cooled, given the prospect of losing southern white support in the upcoming presidential election. Months later, however, the threat of Henry Wallace's Progressive Party candidacy from the left and the defection of southern white Democrats to support Senator Strom Thurmond's challenge from the right as the candidate of the segregationist Dixiecrat Party, appear to have revived Truman's commitment to civil rights by the summer of 1948. Meanwhile A. Philip Randolph had organized an aggressive campaign demanding integration of the armed services, to which Truman acceded, issuing Executive Order 9981 twelve days after he was safely past the Democratic convention's confirmation of his nomination for the presidency. Truman lost four southern states in his razor-thin election victory that fall, but the overwhelming support of northern black voters in Illinois and Ohio may well have tipped the scales toward the Democrats' electoral success.

Thus, less than four decades after its founding convention, the NAACP emerged as a political power player on the American political scene, in large measure thanks to its alliance with the Truman wing of the Democratic Party. It was a status it would seek thereafter to protect above all else. And, indeed, one might credibly argue that this insiders' game of lobbying and legal pressure was validated by its favorable results. The formation of the Leadership Conference on Civil Rights in 1950 consolidated the anti-Communist liberal alliances that had developed over the previous two decades and certainly enhanced the NAACP's role as the premier lobbyist for civil rights policies. Moreover, the presence on staff of Clarence Mitchell, an unusually skilled, Baltimore-based lobbyist, reinforced the organization's Washington-based approach. Consequently, the goal of dismantling school segregation, the success of which would ultimately require decisions in the nation's capital and at the Supreme Court, arguably prioritized the legal strategy Marshall approved rather than the direct-action campaign he condemned. Indeed, it was a strategy that the stream of high-profile legal victories against segregated colleges and universities during the early postwar years appeared to confirm.

On the other hand, in order to sustain its alliance with the Truman White House, the NAACP wholeheartedly embraced the administration's anti-Communist creed, purging its ranks and adopting a more conservative approach and agenda than it had pursued over the previous decade, and consequently shunning many of the progressive groups, allies, and staff that the organization had worked with during the 1930s. Indeed, its dramatic victories coincided, oddly enough, with marked setbacks to earlier successes in expanding black popular support and diminished southern black political empowerment. NAACP membership, which had reached 400,000 by 1945, fell to half that number by the end of 1949, with membership in Tennessee alone dropping from 11,000 to 4,000. Black voter registration in the Deep South also declined. The number of registered black voters plummeted to the point where twenty-four "black belt" counties had none on their rolls at all by 1952. An increasingly common complaint against the organization was that having been drawn to the Washington power game, it had become increasingly distant from the people it purported to serve. By midcentury, the organization that had long epitomized the struggle for racial equality would soon be eclipsed by newer, more militant groups.

These developments were not inevitable: The NAACP had actually been receptive to a broader attack on American racism in years past. As early as 1921, James Weldon Johnson, its first black executive director, declared that "what we need and must have is power"—together, he added in a later speech, with a strategy of "mass action." The architect of the organization's legal assault on segregated schools, Charles Houston, saw no contradiction between political mobilization and the lawyer's role in the courtroom. Recognizing the limits of judicial processes, he believed that ultimately public pressure would be necessary to secure victory in such contentious legal disputes. This was as true, he argued, of the publicity-oriented efforts of the Communist-affiliated defenders of the Scottsboro Boys in the early 1930s as in his own representation of railway workers suing the FEPC in the 1940s. Houston taught his students that the black lawyer must also be a "social engineer." "I am not only a lawyer, but an evangelist and stump speaker," Houston wrote to his protégé Thurgood Marshall in the fall of 1935.

Indeed, Thurgood Marshall appears to have sometimes embraced his mentor's message as well. Black southerners' legal challenges rested first and foremost on their rejection of the humiliation and insult of Jim Crow, he declared at the NAACP meeting in Atlanta in 1951. It was clear to Marshall that such emotional grievances provided the basis for finding plaintiffs willing to fight for their and their children's rights, as well as for mobilizing and securing the support of local communities to sustain them. Mass meetings, the core organizing strategy of later mobilizations, were also the means by which he canvassed communities and secured their support for the organization's legal cases. Thus, on May 28, 1951, when *Briggs v. Elliott* was being argued in Charleston, South Carolina, blacks filled the 150 seats in the courtroom allotted to them while hundreds more spilled into the street outside. They formed an orderly queue along which they passed messages describing the proceedings inside, especially the plaintiffs' arguments, which they applauded. These, then, were not ordinary legal challenges. In fact, they resembled past and future mass mobilizations in support of boycotts, sit-ins, and picket lines.

And yet, Marshall would famously reject civil disobedience as a tactic to achieve social change. Speaking to the NAACP Youth Conference in New Orleans in November 1946, Marshall warned that direct action would lead to "wholesale slaughter with no good achieved." That same year, ironically, Ella Baker, in her role as director of NAACP branches, was leading one of her many leadership-training seminars focused on community organizing. Among her students that year were Rosa Parks and E. D. Nixon, who a decade later inaugurated the first phase of a more militant civil rights movement. Baker's work with the branches took a given community's human resources as her starting point. Presaging the mass movement to come, moreover, she recognized that in southern black communities the church was the "bedrock" on which any organizational initiatives had to build. Then and later, Baker's approach would gain advocates outside the NAACP.

The end of the beginning

Obscured by the NAACP's commitment to a conventional legal strategy and lobbying in Washington, DC, were the parallel campaigns of direct action and confrontation that were surging during those same years. Simultaneous with its progress in school segregation cases during the 1930s and 1940s were protests against racism in department stores by both workers and consumers. The Congress of Racial Equality (CORE) emerged from sit-in protests in Chicago's Loop in 1942. Veterans of CORE, many of whom had studied and were strongly influenced by Gandhi's nonviolent movement in India, would also pioneer the first "freedom ride" to test compliance with the Court-ordered desegregation won by Irene Morgan's lawsuit in 1946.

On April 9, 1947, just six days before Jackie Robinson stepped onto Ebbets Field to become the first black player to integrate professional baseball, Bayard Rustin, George Houser, and fourteen other "freedom riders" left Washington, DC, determined to publicize southern states' continued resistance to the Supreme Court-ordered desegregation of interstate travel. Billing their protest a "Journey of Reconciliation," a term reflecting their belief in the capacity of nonviolent direct action to heal racial tensions as well as challenge racist practices, the group members rehearsed their responses to the confrontations they expected to encounter. And, indeed, although the protests were confined to the Upper South states of Virginia, North Carolina, Tennessee, and Kentucky, the demonstrators did encounter violence and some were imprisoned when they refused to post bail while appealing their convictions for trespass. Bayard Rustin and two others spent twenty-two days on a chain gang. Not only did this protest preview the ideological commitments and tactics of the Civil Rights Movement of later decades, but many of its participants would also go on to mentor a postwar generation born into a world of new expectations and assumptions.

Chapter 2

Communities organizing for change: New South cities

On December 1, 1955, almost exactly a year and a half after the *Brown v. Board of Education* decision shook the nation's racial complacency, a diminutive seamstress, Rosa Parks, refused to relinquish her seat to a white man on a Montgomery, Alabama, bus. Her refusal to obey the etiquette encoded in the region's segregation laws led to her arrest and sparked a fierce, year-long rebellion by Montgomery's black population. Their militancy and unity during the 381-day boycott of the city's buses shook the illusion that blacks willingly accepted the nation's abusive racial order and inspired similar acts of defiance across the South. If one defines the Civil Rights Movement as the mass mobilization of black communities to challenge their racially subordinated civil status, then this was the moment it began.

Parks's initiative and the community mobilization that followed resonated with similar protests stretching back at least a century, from reactions to Elizabeth Jennings's ejection from a horse-drawn carriage in New York in 1854 down to a boycott of motorized buses in Baton Rouge, Louisiana, just two years before Montgomery's. But even though the motivations and tactics of Montgomery's black citizens had much in common with those earlier events, changes in the character of the social relations between the races in Montgomery underscored something different about the conditions of possibility for black resistance at that historic moment. It is significant as well that this postwar movement emerged not in the rural Deep South but in what might be best described as "New South cities"—that is, places where the traditional structures of racial control had begun to unravel during the interwar period and would all but disintegrate in the decade between 1955 and 1965. The old regime did not surrender without a fight, of course, even though city fathers sought to recast their images in more moderate guises. Indeed, some of the bloodiest racial violence and murder in American history stained the nation during the civil rights decade that followed. Under sustained pressure, cities that were ostensibly "too busy to hate," as Atlanta's Ivan Allen Jr. would describe his own metropolis some years later, could and did revert to their old ways. This was especially true of those cities like Montgomery and Birmingham that still straddled the line between the Old and the New South. Nonetheless, it was in such cities—those reshaped by political, economic, and demographic changes during the interwar years—that mass movements were able to mobilize effective pressure for reform. However scarring the white backlash their activism unleashed, it amounted in the end to little more than a rearguard action covering Jim Crow's retreat. The nation had changed; large sectors of the South had changed; and most important, black Americans had changed.

The urban New South

Just eleven years before the Movement erupted in Montgomery, Gunnar Myrdal's groundbreaking study of American race relations, *An American Dilemma*, had implied that the North was the more likely place to launch a successful assault on the Jim Crow racial order. Although the decade of struggle sparked by Rosa Parks's action soon proved him wrong, it was not an unreasonable assumption and likely one shared by many contemporaneous black analysts, some of whom had gathered the data and prepared the working papers Myrdal mined for his study. Indeed, the political changes wrought by demographic and social transformations in the North were already fully evident as Myrdal prepared his final text for publication. Not only were all of the major civil rights advocacy organizations headquartered in northern cities, but so were the most promising mobilizations challenging racial discrimination against black laborers and consumers. During the 1930s, "Don't Buy Where You Can't Work" campaigns had erupted in scores of northern cities from Chicago to Baltimore to New York City, and protesters continued to target department stores in the nation's capital for several years after the Second World War. The interracial labor alliances formed during the late 1930s were strongest in northern cities, in contrast with the dramatic—albeit failing—"Operation Dixie" organizing campaigns that the Congress of industrial Organizations (CIO) launched in Virginia and North Carolina tobacco and cotton factories shortly after the war. And, certainly, the interwar black political renaissance that had flourished in northern cities would provide moral and crucial financial support for the southern-based movement that emerged in the mid-1950s. Nonetheless, contrary to the scenario Myrdal's analysis implied, the decisive breakthroughs in the decades-long civil rights struggle emerged in the urban South.

The migration out of the rural South that had fueled the explosive growth of black communities in northern and western cities had done much the same for southern cities. Indeed, despite the out-migration spurred by the two world wars, in 1950 most black Americans still resided in the ten former slave states of the Confederacy. Montgomery, Birmingham, and Selma in Alabama; Greensboro and Durham in North Carolina; Nashville and Memphis in Tennessee; Atlanta and Albany in Georgia; Baton Rouge, Louisiana; Danville, Virginia; Cambridge, Maryland; and Tallahassee, Florida: these thirteen cities and towns, scattered across the South, would be the focus of the most notable, sustained civil rights protests during the decade framed by the Montgomery boycott in 1955 and the Selma-to-Montgomery march for voting rights in 1965. On average, the populations of these cities were one-third black, although in most the ratio hovered around 40 percent or more. Most black adults in each of these cities were confined to menial jobs, with women heavily concentrated in domestic work. The average number of employed southern black women working as household domestics was rapidly declining, however, from a high of two-thirds in the 1930s to just 40 percent by the 1950s. Commercial laundries absorbed some of these domestic workers, while others found seasonal work in tobacco factories and other industries.

Menial though these urban jobs might have been, they were core features of a dramatic shift in black-white social relations as both the black and white populations in these cities exploded. Urban life and work exposed the fault lines of rural plantation life that since slavery had depended on an intimate (in every sense of the word) relationship between the races, even as it deprived black people of the most basic human dignity. Sharecropping and tenancy labor arrangements often entailed intrusive surveillance of black workers' personal as well as work lives. On many Deep South plantations everything from their diet to their mail could be controlled by their landlord-employers. By contrast, urban modes of life and work entailed greater separation of employment from residence, even for most domestic workers. With greater residential autonomy came greater opportunities to engage in a richer, more varied institutional life than in much of the rural South. Thus urbanization brought freedom of movement, relatively autonomous communication networks, and social infrastructures that would prove crucial to the mass mobilizations that later fueled and sustained the Civil Rights Movement.

Given the stasis of the old regime, the mobilization for war and its aftermath also shook assumptions on both sides of the racial divide. Black veterans returned home ready to fight for freedom on the home front. Some sought to take advantage of the relaxed voter registration requirements for veterans. A few secured G.I. Bill education benefits to get vocational training or attend college, which swelled black college enrollments during the first postwar decade. It is no accident, then, that most of the communities that mobilized during the 1950s and 1960s were adjacent to black college populations that often supplied the shock troops for local protests.

Movement cities also drew on their growing numbers of black high school students, whose very presence was in most cases the result of recently won concessions from municipal administrators. Indeed, in several of these cities the first fruits of black voter mobilizations during the 1940s were provisions for secondary education for their children. Notable as well, many of these early mobilizations occurred in cities that bordered military or naval installations. Although the American military was hardly a conscious agent for social change, the presence of bases reduced the long-standing isolation of southern life and politics from authorities outside the region. Indeed, black workers on military and naval bases often enjoyed privileges denied them in nearby cities. Local civilians were likely aware, for example, that the usual racist tactics of their city policemen were stymied when black servicemen were involved. Moreover, black soldiers in the recently desegregated armed services sometimes conveyed expectations that challenged the entrenched racial conventions of the communities in which they were stationed.

Finally, the urban environment itself entailed both residential separation and cheek-by-jowl interactions between otherwise anonymous blacks and whites in public spaces. This nurtured black solidarity while simultaneously creating multiple flashpoints that exposed racial discrimination and fueled black discontent. It is not surprising, therefore, that bus service—essential for reaching work and leisure in cities—would emerge as a common point of discontent across the region. The century-old grievances about discrimination on common carriers intensified with the increased urbanization of both races by the mid-twentieth century. Unlike long-distance carriers, these intracity bus trips involved a constant churning of the ridership as passengers entered and exited, ensuring a chaotic scramble to sustain an absolute and consistent separation of the races.

Rapid urban growth also intensified discontent around another longstanding grievance: differential and abusive policing. In the late 1940s and early 1950s, simultaneous with the growing unrest on the buses, southern cities witnessed repeated black protests of police misconduct and brutality. The most common abuses enraging black communities were white policemen's sexual assaults against black women. Incidents in Memphis in 1945 and in Montgomery in 1949 and a series of police abuses in Birmingham entrenched those black communities' well-earned skepticism about receiving respect, much less equal justice, from either the police or the courts in those cities.

Montgomery

Although some of the earliest challenges to the southern racial order emerged in cities in the Upper South, where demographic and economic changes were well advanced by the end of World War II, the first community-wide mobilization characteristic of the so-called classic era of civil rights activism emerged in Montgomery, the storied heart and first capital of the Confederacy. By the mid-twentieth century, however, Montgomery had been buffeted by diverse forces that may well have rendered it more vulnerable to change than ostensibly more progressive southern cities. The city's population had grown by 30 percent every decade since 1900, as rural whites and blacks poured into the capital from the Alabama countryside. Consequently, the rough racial parity the city had known for most of the interwar period had given way to a 63 percent white majority by 1955, which ironically destabilized rather than confirmed the political grip of the city's traditional white elite. With civil service reform in 1949 and the emergence of a self-conscious, residentially segregated white working class responsive to insurgent challenges to elite rule, white solidarity was fractured, inadvertently giving blacks a measure of political leverage. Meanwhile, wartime population growth spurred black political activism, producing a seasoned local leadership. In 1943, for example, E. D. Nixon organized the Alabama Voters League, whose registration drives would double the number of black voters by 1955. Given the politically divided white electorate, the city's black minority was able to win important concessions: The city hired black policemen and built two black high schools. Indeed, in 1953 a black newspaper dubbed Montgomery the state's "most enlightened city." It may well have been their sense of steady progress that encouraged the indigenous black leadership's faith in cautious negotiations with the city fathers to address community grievances, including Rosa Parks's arrest.

By 1955, however, forces beyond the city would shape the attitudes of both blacks and whites to the racial status quo. Despite all the dramatic changes in the socioeconomic and cultural infrastructure of the postwar South, the conditions for black advancement and even physical safety in the region remained precarious and fraught. No event made this fact more palpable than the vicious murder in the late summer of that year of fourteen-year-old Emmett Till, a native of Chicago visiting family in the Mississippi Delta. Till's mutilated body was exposed in all its horror by *Jet* magazine, a Chicago-based African American weekly launched in 1951 that was itself a creature of the broader postwar transformation of northern black life. Aided by a newly emergent black media infrastructure, the NAACP publicized the Till lynching and rallied the national black community to protest.

Indeed, just four days before her arrest, Rosa Parks had attended one of the mass meetings protesting Till's murder. Like Carrie Fitzgerald and Irene Morgan a decade earlier, it is clear that her act of defiance on that Cleveland Avenue bus was spontaneous, but only in the sense of being the last straw in a lifetime of suffering callous disrespect. For a number of years Parks had also been engaged in civil rights activities, including a stint as secretary to the local NAACP branch, leadership training from Ella Baker in Jacksonville, Florida, in 1946, and more recently a two-week conference on school desegregation and voter registration at the Highlander Folk School. It is abundantly clear, nonetheless, that she did not anticipate challenging Alabama's segregation laws on that fateful evening. Headed home to the public housing apartment she shared with her husband and aging mother, she had dutifully occupied one of the seats set aside for black passengers. But after an influx of white riders at the Empire Theater stop, the driver moved the sign marking the racial divide and ordered four black passengers to surrender their seats to the new white arrivals. Three blacks moved; Rosa Parks did not. As she explained years later, she did not because she felt "mistreated and humiliated." She also revealed later that the recent Emmett Till atrocity came to mind at that moment, confirming her conviction that she "had been pushed as far as I could stand to be pushed." It was time, she declared, "to know once and for all what rights I had as a human being and a citizen."

Jim Crow had always been degrading and humiliating, of course. As the lawyers for Homer Plessy had argued to challenge its legalization in the 1890s, the segregation of putatively public spaces was nothing less than a "badge of slavery," intended to mark a lower social and moral status for black people and thus inherently insulting. Arguably, as bus systems evolved to serve an even larger public on a daily basis, the humiliation Plessy had felt on a train a half-century earlier grew even more intense. Unlike schools, movie houses, or dining facilities, the economies and geographies of New South cities made buses unavoidable for most working-class white as well as black residents. They became virtual theaters in whose cramped aisles rituals of subordination were reenacted on a daily basis. There for all to see was the raw shaming that the Jim Crow social order inflicted on black people as well as a growing resistance to it. A systematic survey of bus records in nearby Birmingham counted 176 cases of racial

4. This mugshot of Rosa Parks was taken after her second arrest on February 22, 1956, together with nearly a hundred other protesters. Parks's arrest on December 1, 1955, for violating a city ordinance requiring segregated seating on Montgomery buses had sparked a 381-day boycott.

confrontations on that city's buses in a single year, 88 of them involving direct defiance of the city's segregation ordinance. And, most often, the Birmingham resistance, as elsewhere, was from black working-class women. There is no reason to doubt that Montgomery's experience was not similar.

Parks's protest that night was less an objection to being seated in a racially designated separate section of the bus than the insult of being forced to surrender her seat to a white passenger—and to a man at that. Segregation in practice was not simply a matter of separate seating, but the ostentatious marking of one's inferior status, indeed one's literal untouchability. As in many other southern cities, the typical seating arrangement on Montgomery's buses mandated that black passengers occupy the twenty-two seats in the rear, while whites took the fourteen remaining in the front, thus leaving four seats in a veritable "no-man's land," shifting back and forth in order to accommodate ever-changing patterns of white ridership. Indeed, the initial distribution of seats usually reflected the reality that blacks constituted the bulk of the ridership in most cities. Yet whites claimed priority seating at any point when the bus reached capacity. Moreover, the common practice in Montgomery requiring that black riders pay their fare at the front of the bus and then exit to reenter through the rear side door further marked their "untouchable" status. It was not unusual for malicious drivers to leave a stop before a black passenger could reenter the bus. Indeed, this was an indignity to which Rosa Parks had just recently been subjected—by the same driver, Fred Blake, who ordered her to surrender her seat that fateful December night. Thus did black Montgomery share a common visceral anger, less because of racial separation per se than the abuses it authorized.

That widespread anger no doubt goes far to explain the community's unified and immediate response to Parks's arrest. The indignity she suffered resonated across all class and education strata of Montgomery's black community, providing a basis for broad mobilization and action. There had been other women who had challenged segregated seating on the city's buses. In fact, Parks had herself coached Claudette Colvin, a teenage girl arrested under the same statute nine months earlier, but activist leaders had not thought Colvin a suitable plaintiff for a sustained legal campaign. Although Parks's origins, upbringing, and employment were more characteristic of the "respectable" working class than the middle class, her demeanor and reputation appealed to all sectors of Montgomery's black community.

Indeed, the Montgomery movement provides ample evidence of the cross-class dynamic that would make community mobilizations during the civil rights decade so effective. In Montgomery, as in other New South cities, the leadership and organizational infrastructure of the black community was fractured, with each part differing in its makeup and goals. Movement organizers confronted the task of bringing long-established secular and religious organizations as well as a coalition of working-class and middle-class supporters into an effective, if temporarily crisis-driven, organizational alliance. This unusual dynamic is evident in the character of those who responded immediately to Parks's arrest. E. D. Nixon, a veteran of A. Philip Randolph's Brotherhood of Sleeping Car Porters, embodied an ideological link to a black radical working-class tradition stretching back into the 1930s and beyond that was soon to be replicated in other movement cities as older activists mentored and joined with a new generation in the struggle. Most immediately relevant, however, was Nixon's direct involvement, as the local NAACP chair, in recent initiatives to develop a legal challenge to the segregation of Montgomery's buses. Working in parallel with Nixon, the Women's Political Council was an activist group made up mainly of Alabama State College faculty, led by an English professor, Jo Ann Robinson. The staunchly middle-class Council had also been agitating for some time to end segregated seating on the city's buses. Acting independently, Nixon rushed to Parks's house as soon as he heard of her arrest and convinced her to file a legal test case. Meanwhile, Robinson and other black women faculty worked well into the night drafting and mimeographing a call for a one-day bus boycott.

As Nixon well knew, however, the crucial institutional basis for mobilizing a southern black community was its churches, which were a veritable minefield of personal and institutional rivalries, secular ambitions, and arcane doctrinal differences. Gaining the support of this fractious group would require vesting its leadership in a nondenominational ministerial alliance. Nixon claimed, in retrospect, the additionally brilliant insight of getting the ministers to select a relative newcomer, Martin Luther King Jr., as the alliance's leader. Thus did twenty-six-year-old Martin King Jr.—a recent recipient of a Boston University doctorate and, far more important, the son and namesake of one of the South's most prominent Baptist ministers—emerge on the national scene. The younger King's remarkable ability to fuse the idioms and cadences of indigenous black religion with a lofty philosophical discourse, drawn from a diverse array of thinkers from Thoreau to Gandhi, made him an exceptional national spokesperson for the emerging movement. Not only was King uniquely suited to the task of consolidating the cross-class alliance that Parks's arrest had triggered, but his sermons also invested a protest that had emerged out of visceral anger and frustration with historical, civic, and moral purpose. Equally important, perhaps, King's seeming humility and unflappable confidence likely enabled him to negotiate the notorious egos and factiousness of the black ministers forming the leadership alliance.

Nonetheless, Martin Luther King Jr. was as much follower as leader when he took the stage at Holt Street Baptist Church two days after Parks's arrest. Certainly nothing in his prior experience, training, or upbringing would have prepared him for such a radical challenge to the southern way of life. Indeed, he needed to look no farther than his own father's career path in Atlanta to be reminded of the institutional limits, the desire to sustain social respectability and class position, and the sheer precariousness of ministerial careers in the black South, all of which conspired to encourage a cautious conservatism among most black ministers as well as other civic leaders. Thus it was no doubt the palpable enthusiasm and determination of the people he led that turned King from just another ambitious young preacher into the iconic prophet of a mass movement.

Ministers and their churches brought more than a readily formed mass of followers to the Movement, however. Few other community institutions offered black people the opportunity to develop the organizational skills that would prove crucial to sustaining a consumer boycott. The boycott movement confronted diverse logistical challenges, such as providing rapid and efficient communication over a months-long campaign in a community where few people had phone service and black newspapers had infrequent editions. Thus the face-to-face and word-of-mouth contacts at church meetings proved essential, even when supplemented by contacts through social clubs and other organizations able to produce mimeographed flyers. Church-based organizations provided as well the contacts and venues for addressing the formidable logistical problems posed by the boycott. If the people who had depended on buses to get to work were to now withhold their patronage for a sustained period of time, they needed alternative means of transportation. Through contacts already established through the National Baptist Council, King and other ministers in Montgomery knew and sought the counsel of Rev. Theodore J. Jemison, an officer of the council, who had himself led the brief bus boycott in Baton Rouge, Louisiana, just two and a half years earlier and touted it as a blueprint for other cities.

There were important differences between Baton Rouge and Montgomery, however. Bus operations in Baton Rouge were much more vulnerable to a black boycott than most cities, given its 80 percent black ridership, and its white political leadership had proved somewhat less obdurate than elsewhere. Most important, the Baton Rouge boycott lasted only two weeks, ending with what many believed to be an unsatisfactory compromise. Thus the difficulties and full potential of a mobilized community had not been fully tested there. Nonetheless, although the Movement did not begin in Baton Rouge, its experience did offer Montgomery's leaders valuable lessons in how to organize an alternative to the buses and the church-based local financing that would sustain a much longer protest.

Drawing on Jemison's experience, Montgomery's leaders called at first on the city's black taxi drivers to provide rides at cut-rate fares, but they eventually had to abandon that solution when confronted by the city's legal interdictions. Montgomery's boycott leaders then turned to a volunteer car pool, but the task soon proved far more formidable than the 150 car owners Jemison had signed up in Baton Rouge. The Montgomery car pool had to replace the 30,000 to 40,000 fares that the bus company was losing each day, which translated into 20,000 rides each day, or about 130 rides per available car. Supplying fuel and maintenance posed a considerable financial and managerial challenge, and the boycott campaign was further inhibited by police harassment of both the riders and their drivers, the first accosted for "loitering" at pickup locations and the latter issued traffic tickets for petty, often phantom infractions.

As in Baton Rouge, the initial demands of the Montgomery movement were not for integration at all but simply seating on a first-come, first-served basis. Their demands were consistent with and a reflection of the visceral anger that had sparked Parks's defiance and the community's initial response: End the humiliating insults inherent in the existing system rather than racial separation per se. Specifically, black Montgomery wanted a firm boundary between the races that did not require blacks to surrender seats to whites, a goal an uncomprehending Roy Wilkins and others at the NAACP would dismiss as simply a "more polite segregation." The protesters also demanded both greater courtesy from all drivers and the employment of black drivers for predominantly black routes, anticipating that this, too, would ensure more humane treatment.

The putatively conservative demands of the early boycotts reflect an irony that has gone largely unrecognized. Although the Civil Rights Movement mobilized under the banner of ending racial segregation of national life, not only did black communities approach that goal with some ambivalence, but also the protest movement itself was enabled by the very institutions nurtured by the informal as well as the legally mandated separation of the races; most notably its churches and schools. It was not immediately plausible to a majority of black southerners that integration as such would be an effective solution to the inequities they confronted on a daily basis. It was equally clear, however, that black people saw clear distinctions between a separation they chose and their rejection of the daily humiliations of the involuntary segregation white authorities imposed on them. White southerners met even modest demands with intransigence and violence, however, thus muddying the distinction between the *separation* blacks chose and the *segregation* they loathed. Arguably, then, the intransigent and even violent response of southern whites to the prospect of even a "more polite segregation" helped make integration a desirable goal.

Membership in the White Citizens Council, formed in the context of the campaign of "massive resistance" to the *Brown v. Board of Education* decision, had skyrocketed from six hundred to twelve thousand. The homes of Movement leaders, including King and E. D. Nixon, were bombed. White Montgomery's political leaders, as well as those at the state level, became more recalcitrant. Although the boycott had a devastating impact on the soon-bankrupted bus company, which was owned by a Chicago-based firm, the city fathers blocked any move to negotiate a settlement.

In the end, therefore, as NAACP lawyers liked to point out, the final victory was achieved, as they preferred, through a court in Washington rather than on the streets of Montgomery. Fred Gray, then only a year out of law school, had filed a suit on February 1, 1956, that led to a successful Supreme Court decision nine months later. Gray's suit was not based on the original criminal case arising out of Rosa Parks's arrest, however, because of fears that her suit would become entangled in delays in the state courts, thus putting off for years a decisive reckoning in the US Supreme Court. Consequently, the decisive victory came with *Browder v. Gayle*, a case brought by Aurelia Browder, the lead plaintiff, against William A. Gayle, the mayor of Montgomery. The *Browder* case was built on a string of arrests of women very much like Rosa Parks, black women who had been charged under the same segregation ordinance during the nine months preceding Parks's arrest. Mary Louise Smith and Claudette Colvin were teenagers—eighteen and fifteen, respectively. Browder and Susie McDonald, thirty-six and seventy, were older, as was another plaintiff, Jeanette Reese, a domestic worker who dropped out after being intimidated by unidentified whites. Their relatively young ages or their elders' less vulnerable occupations may explain the motivations of the women who persisted in the suit. Susie McDonald was a widow living off the pension left by her deceased husband, who like E. D. Nixon had been a railroad employee. Browder's education and political activism were very similar to Rosa Parks's. Having been mentored by Jo Ann Robinson when she was a student at Alabama State College, Browder had joined the local NAACP chapter and participated in its voter registration campaigns. On June 5, arguing that state enforcement of racial discrimination violated the equal protections guaranteed by the Fourteenth Amendment, the plaintiffs won a two-to-one decision in federal district court, where the legendary southern liberal judge Frank Johnson presided. Six months later, on December 17, that decision was affirmed by the US Supreme Court.

Despite NAACP sneers, what Montgomery showed—as Charles Houston would have readily recognized—was that a successful attack on Jim Crow required *both* direct action and legal strategies working in tandem, rather than at cross-purposes. The Montgomery Movement mobilized not only that community but also the nation's black citizenry as a whole. Even though final victory came via a court decision, it was not lost on ordinary black Americans that Montgomery residents had demonstrated their capacity for unified and disciplined collective action despite economic intimidation and extreme violence. In its aftermath, the commitment to direct action grew stronger, especially among young people. Indeed, the *Browder* decision also ensured the success of a bus boycott in Tallahassee that had been launched the previous spring by students at Florida A&M and Rev. Charles Steele, a minister who had recently moved there from Montgomery.

Greensboro and Nashville

On Monday, February 1, 1960, Ezell Blair Jr., Franklin McCain, Joseph McNeil, and David Richmond, all freshmen at North Carolina Agricultural and Technical University in Greensboro, calmly took seats at the lunch counter of the local Woolworth's. Their bold action sparked a new, even more dramatic phase in the direct-action movement initiated by the Montgomery bus boycott, an event they would have witnessed as high school freshmen. Much like the Montgomery boycott, the historical significance of their act was not that it was unprecedented. Not only did the sit-in tactic also have a long history stretching back to the nineteenth century, but it had also been deployed more recently in St. Louis, Missouri; in Oklahoma City; and by an NAACP-affiliated youth group in Wichita, Kansas. These cases reflected the greater militancy of local NAACP chapters that were often in conflict with the organization's more conservative national leadership.

5. In February 1960 Ronald Martin, Robert Patterson, and Mark Martin staged a sit-in after being refused service at F. W. Woolworth's lunch counter in Greensboro, North Carolina. This was part of the wave of sit-ins sparked by four students from North Carolina A&T earlier that month.

A New South city like Greensboro offered greater opportunities for the successful deployment of this tactic than northern and border states, however. The rapidity of its adoption and the character of the cities to which sit-ins immediately spread underscore how and why the events in Greensboro became iconic of a new phase in the equal rights struggle. The original "Greensboro Four" were joined by nineteen of their fellow students the very next day; by the end of the week their numbers had grown to four hundred and spread to a Woolworth's competitor, S. H. Kress & Co. Within two months, the protest had spread to more than thirty-one southern cities in eight states; by summer the numbers affected had grown larger still.

It is perhaps telling that the greatest concentration of the initial sit-in protests was in the cities clustered around Greensboro and in Nashville, Tennessee. Both areas were exemplary of the social and demographic transformations of the postwar decades, especially the growth of black secondary school populations and the concentration of black college students. The Greensboro sit-ins drew support locally from Dudley High School, which had opened in 1929, the first high school for blacks in the county, and two black colleges—North Carolina AT&T and Bennett, a historically black women's college. The protests were soon joined by three intrepid white supporters from the Woman's College of the University of North Carolina. Eventually, students from black colleges in nearby cities, Durham, Winston-Salem, and Charlotte, swelled their numbers further before bringing the protests to their own cities. Nashville protesters also came principally from that city's four black colleges—Fisk University, Meharry Medical College, Tennessee State Agricultural and Industrial College, and the American Baptist Theological Seminary. Their numbers were augmented by black secondary school students from Nashville's Pearl High School, which was itself the fruit of an earlier generation's political activism. The relatively progressive image of these cities was often reflected in the self-conscious promotional campaigns of their white political establishment's commitment to greater economic development, which made them wary of overt racial conflict. Moreover, the targets of the sit-ins were usually branches or franchises of national corporations vulnerable to outside pressure. Consequently, although local white popular resistance might be fierce, even violent, it would not necessarily be decisive.

In Nashville, for example, the activists were reputedly treated at first more like annoyances than lawbreakers. Indeed, through a rigorously disciplined nonviolent approach, the Nashville movement succeeded in desegregating six downtown lunch counters, with the exception ironically of Woolworth's, which held out until 1965. By contrast, progress was slower in Greensboro and many other cities and did not happen at all in Deep South cities like Jackson, Mississippi. Nonetheless, most lunch counters in five-and-ten chain stores in Upper South states like Virginia,

Tennessee, Maryland, and North Carolina were eventually desegregated. The national impact of their success encouraged many of the postwar youth coming of age in the early 1960s to commit themselves to a long direct-action struggle against the South's Jim Crow regime.

The spontaneous initiatives of the younger generation, moreover, drew support from some of their elders, among whom were veterans of direct-action initiatives in northern and border cities a decade earlier, as well as others who had grown impatient with the elite-focused strategies of the NAACP. Thus Greensboro students found support from Floyd McKissick, the NAACP Youth Council leader in Durham. McKissick, in turn, called on Gordon Carey of CORE, who had been involved in a sit-in protest in Miami the previous year. Martin Luther King Jr., now heading the Southern Christian Leadership Conference (SCLC), also offered support. The movement continued to receive support from some local white students, as well as most prominently, from the National Student Association, harbingers of similar individual and institutional support forthcoming later that decade. By contrast, the national NAACP (as opposed to its local chapters) kept its distance from the students, even going so far as refusing to defend the first group arrested in Greensboro. Although that position would soon become politically unsustainable, given broad popular support of the sit-in movement, the organization's skepticism of—and sometimes outright hostility to—direct-action tactics persisted, nonetheless.

James Lawson, a student at Vanderbilt's Divinity School, was among the cohort of activists from the previous generation who, like James Farmer and Bayard Rustin, had been converted to Gandhian nonviolence as a personal moral conviction as well as a political tactic. In contrast with Greensboro and other protest centers, Lawson had been organizing workshops in Nashville since 1959, from which disciplined teams of protesters scattered every Saturday to stage sit-ins in downtown department stores, having undergone rigorous training in nonviolent tactics before attacking Jim Crow lunch counters. Not only did the Nashville Movement succeed in integrating several lunch counters, therefore, but it also produced a cadre of trained young leaders—Diane Nash, John Lewis, James Bevel, Bernard Lafayette, Marion Barry, and C. T. Vivian—who would profoundly shape the course of the Movement across the South. All but Vivian, moreover, would be among the founders of the Student Nonviolent Coordinating Committee (SNCC, or more colloquially "Snick"), which soon became the lodestar for the youth cadres of the growing equal rights movement over the next decade.

Native South Carolinian Septima Clark, sixty-two years old and a veteran of voter registration campaigns over the previous decade, was among the first adult activists to recognize the potential of this cadre of activist youth. In early April 1960, she hosted a weekend conference at the Highlander Folk School for about a hundred students drawn from nineteen states, all of whom had been active in local sit-in protests. Their meeting may be remembered best for folk singer Guy Carawan's introduction of his version of "We Shall Overcome," a song based on an African American hymn from the pre-gospel era that had been adapted by white union organizers in the 1930s. What Clark initiated was continued two weeks later when many of the students who had attended the Highlander meeting moved on to Shaw University in Raleigh, North Carolina, for an even more consequential gathering. There, Ella Baker, another veteran organizer from the previous generation, brought together 150 participants from nine states, not simply to share their sit-in experiences but also to create an independent youth-led civil rights organization, SNCC. Marion Barry, a veteran of Lawson's Nashville Movement, was elected SNCC's first national chairman, and other Nashville veterans formed its initial core. Although Baker had prevailed on King's SCLC to fund the conference and provide quarters for its office in a corner of its own small Atlanta headquarters, she also insisted that the students maintain a separate organizational identity and independence from adult dictates.

Given the prominent role the Nashville group played during the first phase of its existence, SNCC's primary focus was, unsurprisingly, on organizing civil disobedience campaigns in New South cities. Having been evicted from the SCLC offices after Baker was replaced by Wyatt T. Walker, Jane Stembridge, SNCC's lone staff member, decided to undertake a recruitment trip through the rural South in the company of newly arrived SCLC volunteer Bob Moses, then a schoolteacher in New York City. During that trip Moses met Amzie Moore, a Mississippi activist, whose pleas for assistance with voter registration in that state had hitherto fallen on deaf ears. Their collaboration would in time lead SNCC to engage in a very different kind of community organizing.

The road to Mississippi and the re-envisioning of movement tactics and goals would run first through Deep South cities like Montgomery and Birmingham, however, both of which straddled the Old South–New South divide more than the sites of the earlier sit-ins. Eventually, the struggle for equal access to public accommodations would shift to different, more challenging terrains, as well. For the moment, however, Irene Morgan's fateful trip from northern Virginia to Baltimore two decades earlier still hung over the quest for equal citizenship. Both the courts and the Interstate Commerce Commission (ICC) had ruled repeatedly that interstate travelers were entitled to equal treatment not only on buses but also in the terminal facilities that accommodated the travelers; the commission had been laggard in enforcing that mandate, however, until pressured by the US Supreme Court's *Boynton v. Virginia* decision in December 1960 and by the Kennedy Justice Department. In the aftermath of that decision, CORE decided to reprise its Journey of Reconciliation tactic and once again press for enforcement of the ICC's now decade-old mandate. Led by James Farmer, the recently elected head of

CORE, the Freedom Riders would retrace the route through the Upper South of the earlier journey, but this time continue on through the Deep South as well. Nashville veteran John Lewis joined the protesters training at the launch point in Washington, DC. On May 4, two interracial groups boarded two buses, one on the Trailways line and the other on Greyhound, and departed Washington for New Orleans. Many of them were already veterans of the sit-in movement, but their upcoming journey was destined to transform once more the character of the still evolving Civil Rights Movement.

Chapter 3

Communities organizing for change: The new "Old South"

Having boarded a Greyhound bus in Washington, DC, bound for New Orleans on May 4, 1961, CORE-sponsored Freedom Riders set out to test yet again southern compliance with federal mandates requiring an end to racial discrimination in interstate travel. With the exception of an assault on John Lewis in Rock Hill, South Carolina, the first stage of the riders' journey was comparatively peaceful, until they reached Anniston, Alabama. There they confronted the first signs of having entered another South. Mobs attacked them and their bus was burned. Unhinged mob violence continued in Montgomery and then again in Birmingham, where police deliberately held back to allow the mob time to do its bloody work, which included viciously beating the riders at the bus station and threatening to storm the church where they later sought refuge. With the local police complicit in the violence and the Justice Department unable—and often unwilling—to spend the political capital necessary to effectively enforce the court's mandate and protect the riders, the original group abandoned its plan to continue on to New Orleans. At that point, Diane Nash, a veteran of the Nashville sit-ins, mobilized a new group determined to complete the journey. With the Alabama Guard escorting them out of the state, the riders finally reached the dreaded Mississippi border, shortly after which they were arrested and jailed. Unwittingly no doubt, their journey now foreshadowed one that the Movement itself would eventually take: from New South to Old.

After a brief incarceration in Jackson, they were taken to Parchman prison farm, where they endured a months-long gulag-like experience that made the city jails of Nashville, Greensboro, and even Montgomery look civilized by comparison. As so often happened, the systematic campaign of physical and psychological abuse in the jailhouse backfired, not only failing to break the protesters' spirits but allowing them instead to forge personal bonds and commitments that would fuel an even fiercer future assault against an increasingly terrorist regime. The Freedom Riders emerged from Parchman a battle-hardened corps determined to wage an unrelenting assault against the South's Jim Crow order. Nonetheless, they were likely unaware that their journey to Parchman would mark a new phase of the Movement. Their confrontations over access to public accommodations would soon give way to life-and-death struggles over political power, thus addressing the very essence of black Americans' now century-old claim to citizenship: the right to vote. Ironically, then, these protests inadvertently marked a return to first principles, to the core demands of the antiracist agitation of the 1940s and, indeed, of the previous century.

Not unrelated to this turn, Movement activists would soon learn, was the realization that the Old South posed challenges quite different from those they had faced in New South cities like Nashville and Greensboro. In those cities, an economic and political white elite, intent on modernizing their social image without upsetting the racial order, had proved somewhat vulnerable to consumer boycotts, sit-ins, and street demonstrations. The viability of such protests had been evident to some degree even in Montgomery, the birthplace of the Confederacy, despite the political gravity of a reactionary state administration pulling it toward a recalcitrance that only the federal courts would break. It was fitting, then, that at this historical turning point the two cities targeted by the Movement shortly after the Freedom Rides—Albany, Georgia, and Birmingham, Alabama—also sat on the regional and temporal fissure separating New South from Old, each reflecting fierce attachments to the half-century-old Jim Crow regime even as they were being buffeted by the demographic transformations and changing social infrastructures characteristic of New South cities: new transportation networks feeding a more diverse economy, military bases forging unsettling links both to federal authority and the broader world beyond, and black college campuses that could serve as relatively safe havens for and incubators of resistance.

The Albany movement

With a population of almost fifty-six thousand, 36 percent of whom were black, Albany, Georgia, might have seemed an unlikely staging ground for the more militant mass street demonstrations phase of the Movement that began in the early 1960s. Situated like its namesake, the capital city of New York, on an economically strategic river, Georgia's Albany had thrived originally by serving the cotton economy. By the interwar period, however, it had diversified its industrial base, with seven rail lines supplementing its original reliance on transport via the Flint River, making the city one of the most important transportation hubs in the South. Social as well as economic changes in the area were intensified by the buildup of military infrastructure during World War II. Much of that largess flowed south thanks to the region's control of key congressional committees, the bounty of the institutional seniority gained through the disfranchisement of black voters. Thus did Georgia's ill-gotten congressional muscle bless its southwest corner with multiple military installations—a US Air Corps base established in the 1940s and a Marine Corps installation in the early 1950s. Given the resultant influx of white residents, Albany's black inhabitants, who had been a majority before the war, constituted a somewhat smaller share of the city's population by 1960. The men were still concentrated in unskilled labor while half the women worked as domestics in white households. Consequently, as in most Movement cities, the initiative for change would spring from the area's growing college and high school student populations, both relatively free of the economic and social constraints felt by most of their elders. Inspired by W. E. B. Du Bois's *Souls of Black Folk*, a black educator had founded an institute to train teachers there in 1903. Forty years later, that institute, having achieved state support and collegiate status, was renamed Albany State College. As with similar institutions elsewhere in the South, the postwar decades witnessed dramatic growth in Albany State's student population.

When twenty-five-year-old Charles Sherrod and nineteen-year-old Cordell Reagon arrived in Albany in November 1961, therefore, they were greeted expectantly by some of these students as "Freedom Riders." Although the characterization was true of Reagon, a Nashville native who had made the journey from Montgomery to Jackson, the Virginia native Charles Sherrod's first Movement experience had been his recent arrest and sentence to thirty days at hard labor for a sit-in demonstration in Rock Hill, South Carolina. They were both familiar with Bob Moses's ongoing voter registration initiatives in Mississippi, however, and had come to begin a similar project in Dougherty County.

As often happened with SNCC field workers, however, upon moving their operations to the county seat in Albany their initial agenda was overtaken by developments on the ground. The students they attracted wanted to challenge the still-segregated waiting rooms and lunch counters at the Trailways bus station. An Albany State College student had been arrested earlier for attempting to eat at the bus terminal's "white" restaurant during a trip home. Rejecting the opposition of older leaders, especially the head of the local NAACP chapter, the students launched a sit-in campaign that led to arrests and school expulsions, all of which eventually brought their more reticent parents into the conflict as well. Within two weeks 267 people had been jailed, a figure destined to rise as the crisis deepened.

In order to negotiate the tensions between rival organizations that were typical of such mobilizations, William Anderson, a college friend of SCLC's Ralph Abernathy, formed an umbrella organization, the Albany Movement. As president, Anderson urged the organization to invite Martin Luther King Jr. to support its efforts. The presence of King, who had recently been featured on the cover of *Time* magazine, would bring not only national attention and resources, they hoped, but also increased local support from black adults. And, indeed, arrests soon reached 750 a week, which taxed city resources as well as jail space, since hundreds of demonstrators chose to not post bail. The no-bail tactic had been used a year earlier by the eleven demonstrators, including Sherrod and Diane Nash, arrested in Rock Hill, South Carolina, and before that by the original Freedom Riders in the 1940s. After Albany, it became a frequent tactic deployed to pressure local authorities by filling local jails beyond capacity. As Movement tactics moved from small cohorts of sit-in demonstrators to the mass street marches of hundreds at a time, the threat of filling the jails became much more plausible. And, indeed, the "jail-ins" soon exhausted Albany's resources, leading the city to send prisoners to nearby county jails where conditions were harsher and beatings frequent, especially at the notorious Baker County jail.

The Albany Movement pioneered another tactical innovation when SNCC workers discovered the power of music to motivate and consolidate a mass audience's solidarity and commitment. Drawing on familiar religious ideas and idioms to express a collective commitment and courage, the emerging music of the Movement provided a language of resistance capable of uniting a black community that might otherwise splinter along class and generational divides. It could literally give voice to ordinary people, thereby reversing the conventional power relations of preacher and audience. In contrast with the disciplined silence of a sit-in and even the communal bonding familiar lyrics could inspire during a mass meeting, music became the veritable armor enveloping protest actions, bringing group discipline and reinforcing individual commitment. Thanks to the discovery in Albany of the extraordinary talents of two local preachers' daughters, Rutha Harris and Bernice Johnson, SNCC formed the Freedom Singers, which became a key fundraiser for the organization as well as messengers to mobilize latent white and black support throughout the nation.

Although the mobilization of ordinary people ready not only to march in support of their demands for freedom and justice but also to spend long stints in jail was unprecedented and magnificent, it soon faltered on all-too-familiar fault lines of such broad-based mobilizations. The Montgomery Movement had shown that an aroused community could sustain a months-long consumer boycott, because fundamentally it amounted to an act of noncooperation rather than direct confrontations with authorities. The Freedom Riders had further proved that a small, disciplined corps of protesters could endure long stints in jail, notwithstanding the alternation between demoralizing boredom and brutal physical assaults. By contrast, mass marches and jail-with-no-bail required more than most adults, living on the edge of subsistence, could be expected to sustain. No doubt, the need for quick victories may have been a factor leading Albany's traditional leaders to invite the now-famous King to join their struggle. King's presence did in fact bring national attention to the Albany struggle and enliven local participation. But, then, as later, it was in fundamental contradiction with the philosophy that enduring movements had to be built from the bottom up and not depend on charismatic leadership. That was among the reasons SNCC's new chairman, James Forman, had opposed the decision to invite King to Albany, opening a fissure between SNCC and

SCLC that would never be fully closed. However, the viability of SCLC itself was often dependent on King's presence and fundraising capacity. Neither SNCC nor SCLC ever entirely resolved these dilemmas.

King had his own dilemmas as well, since sustaining the media's attention required continuous conflict and crisis, preferably headline-grabbing violence and, regrettably, bloodshed. By the same token, a strategy overly dependent on national media attention was vulnerable to Cold War distractions, like the Berlin Crisis between June and late November 1961 and the Cuban Missile Crisis in October 1962. These came at the very moments the Albany Movement was struggling to sustain its momentum.

Given this climate, King's political leverage was often further weakened once he was out of jail and thus deprived of the attention that the domestic crisis his jailing had created. In Albany, for example, when King was forced to renege on his no-bail pledge—in one case because he was bailed out by an anonymous benefactor against his wishes and in another when he was forced to leave because of the mental health crisis of a fellow inmate—he lost face with his most radical followers for what seemed his lack of resolve. At another point during the Albany campaign he confronted the absurdity of the national press actually praising Albany's police chief Laurie Pritchett for his nonviolent "restraint" and efficiency, while denigrating King as irresolute and inept.

Eventually King settled for a face-saving exit from Albany, justified by the mayor's suspect pledge to obey the ICC's nondiscrimination edict if King left town. The city reneged on that commitment, but by that time the Albany Movement was unable to recover the intensity and unity of its earlier protests. Unable to achieve any of its original goals, therefore, the Albany Movement was henceforth branded by some as an abject failure. Others firmly rejected that assessment, however. Under the leadership of

Charles Sherrod, who eventually settled in the city and made a permanent commitment to it, SNCC continued the painstaking work of voter registration and community organization that had been its original goal. Meanwhile, as Albany faded from newspaper coverage, King's leadership capacities were questioned for the first time.

SCLC would draw on its perceived mistakes in Albany as it planned the Birmingham campaign it launched the following year. Buttressed by a strong, indigenous SCLC leadership that had been long active in that city, the organization would carefully control the preparation and timing of the protest campaign there. In fact, King had already initiated planning with local leaders during a visit to the city in early December 1962.

Birmingham

With a population of 340,887, Birmingham was—after Atlanta and Memphis—the third largest southern city where there was significant Movement activity during the "classic" Movement era. Since the late nineteenth century, it had been one of the South's industrial centers, anchored like its British namesake in the iron and steel industry, which meant a greater dependence on outside capital, more labor union activity, and the growth of a substantial black middle class that was second only to Atlanta's in its exceptional institutional and financial resources. Blacks made up 40 percent of the city's population in 1960 and more than a third of its workforce. Although 42 percent of black women were still relegated to domestic labor—and thus to paternalistic relations that might inhibit their participation in protests—that figure was far lower than the three-quarters similarly occupied there thirty years earlier; moreover, it was still declining.

As in Montgomery, economic development created tensions between the city's ostensibly progressive white elite and an increasingly reactionary white faction of diehard racists opposed to yielding any quarter to the city's black citizens. Most prominent among the latter faction was public safety commissioner Eugene "Bull" Connor, who earned his nickname breaking labor unions in the 1930s. Connor's recent re-election by a landslide 66 percent of the vote signaled the difficult political terrain the Birmingham Movement would confront in the spring of 1963.

The political struggle among the city's white factions proved both an aid and a complication for Movement strategy. Unlike Albany's police chief, Laurie Pritchett, "Bull" Connor's reaction to the Freedom Riders had already revealed a man whose uninhibited violence was sure to produce a crisis that would attract sympathetic world attention to the protesters' demands. Even unsympathetic white observers recognized that the Movement was challenging an anachronistic racial regime. Unlike the earlier sit-in protests, moreover, the intended audience for these demonstrations was a federal government embroiled more deeply than ever in a Cold War competition for world influence. The Movement's strategy, therefore, was to mobilize political pressure for change by focusing on a literal "demonstration" of Jim Crow's injustices. Although this seemed a sensible alternative to the generally disappointing results of negotiations with local authorities that had been attempted in Albany and Montgomery, its unintended consequence was the lessened emphasis on the slow and painstaking work of community organization advocated by Movement veterans like Ella Baker. Indeed, in a short while, this would cause an even deeper schism between SNCC and SCLC.

In early December 1962, the SCLC brain trust gathered in Birmingham for a secret planning meeting with Rev. Fred Shuttlesworth and other local allies. They saw Birmingham as an even more favorable target than most New South cities because its steel mills and associated enterprises made it vulnerable to pressure from northern corporate powers, which might be leveraged to push for concessions to Movement demands, as had been the case when earlier sit-ins targeted national chain stores.

Moreover, there were fewer competing black groups in the city that might complicate decisions about strategy and tactics: The NAACP had been outlawed in Alabama following the *Brown* decision and SNCC and CORE had never been active there. The organizers did encounter opposition from some members of the local black elite, including the millionaire banker A. G. Gaston, the conservative newspaper editor C. A. Scott, and a local minister, Rev. J. L. Ware. But Shuttlesworth had full control of the local umbrella ministerial group, the Alabama Christian Movement for Human Rights, that would plan and oversee operations.

Drawing on the recent Albany experience, SCLC designed a four-stage protest that would build gradually from an initial Christmas boycott of downtown businesses to small-scale sit-ins that winter to a climax of mass street marches designed to fill the jails. At that point there would be a national call for outside participants similar to the Freedom Riders, who would enable the leaders to send hundreds of demonstrators at a time committed to spend at least five or six days in jail, thus creating a decisive crisis. Meanwhile celebrities like Sammy Davis Jr. and Harry Belafonte would be recruited to give fundraising concerts to pay the bail and legal fees crucial to sustaining a lengthy campaign.

The original plan encountered an unexpected complication when the mayoral election pitting the reactionary "Bull" Connor against a reputedly more moderate Albert Boutwell required a runoff. Although Boutwell won the runoff on April 2 and was inaugurated on April 15, Connor refused to concede, leading to a legal battle that further delayed resolution of the electoral deadlock. The political stalemate thwarted ongoing efforts by Birmingham businessmen Sidney Smyer and David Vann, who had formed a secret group to negotiate a solution with their black bourgeois counterparts, attorney Arthur Shores and banker A. G. Gaston. Pressured to put off what some black as well as white observers considered "untimely" protests given the unresolved mayoral

6. On May 4, 1963, hundreds of black grade-school children spilled out of Birmingham's Sixteenth Street Baptist Church to form a "Children's March" against racism. As they approached city hall, they were arrested and herded to the city jail.

contest, King responded with an eloquent defense describing a century-long delay that black Americans had already endured waiting for "the new birth of freedom" that Lincoln had promised a century earlier.

Targeting the Easter shopping season, the boycott was intensified and street demonstrations accelerated, shifting the focus in early April from picketing downtown merchants to mass marches on city hall. Having exhausted the adults available and willing to fill the jails, however, the pace of demonstrations faltered as the numbers volunteering for arrest plunged from thousands to tens. While King was out of town, Nashville veteran James Bevel decided to mobilize elementary as well as high school and college students to revive the street demonstrations. On May 2, thousands of young people, marching two abreast and organized into successive waves of fifty at a time, burst from Shuttlesworth's Sixteenth Street Baptist Church. Although the tactic was

62

condemned at first by many black as well as white observers, it eventually turned the public against Connor's recalcitrance.

Once the city's jails filled to capacity, Connor changed tactics, deploying high-pressure firehoses and dogs to intimidate demonstrators rather than arresting them. The hoses were rigged to give the water explosive force by channeling it from two hoses through a single nozzle, which produced enough force to knock bricks loose from buildings. Children were sent reeling, and scores required hospital treatment in the aftermath of these assaults. The tactic backfired. The brutalization of young children deepened the black community's support for the Movement, and national and international newspaper and television coverage created a public relations nightmare for the city. The Kennedy administration, which had heretofore been reluctant to intervene, was discomfited as well because the images provided powerful

7. **Birmingham police attack child demonstrators in Kelly Ingram Park with high-pressure fire hoses in May 1963. Not only did these demonstrations increase the number of adult protesters, but violence against children also aroused national opposition to the city's racial policies.**

propaganda advantages to the Soviet Union and drew angry protests from several newly independent African nations. Among the most powerful of these images was an iconic image taken by AP photographer Bill Hudson, showing a policeman in dark glasses grasping Walter Gadsden while he was being attacked by a police dog. It was later discovered that Gadsden, a Parker High School student and relative of C. A. Scott, the conservative editor of the *Birmingham World* and, ironically, a fierce critic of King and the demonstrations, was actually a bystander rather than a participant in the demonstration. Nonetheless, the photograph appeared in the *New York Times* the following morning, horrifying none other than the president of the United States. Thus, federal and local pressures for a settlement intensified, leading the city to agree to the protesters' demands on May 10, just six months after King had abandoned Albany.

After Birmingham

The summer following the Birmingham protests witnessed an unprecedented wave of civil rights protests across the nation. Almost immediately after the settlement there, protests and police violence exploded in Danville, Virginia, an Albany-sized center of cotton mills and tobacco factories sixty miles north of Greensboro. Like Danville, most of the protest cities that mobilized thereafter shared at least some similarities with Nashville, Greensboro, Montgomery, Albany, and Birmingham. Whether large or small, their economic, political, and demographic features were similar, while diverging significantly from the regional pattern. All had seen significant population growth—black and white—since the First World War. Most important, their black citizens' grievances were the same as those that had angered Carrie Fitzgerald, Irene Morgan, Rosa Parks, and countless anonymous others: the daily humiliation of encounters in public spaces that southern urban economies produced—on city buses, at lunch counters, and in department stores. It was not that these were the most objectively important issues black southerners faced; denial of municipal and industrial jobs, the right to vote, and justice in courts of law would have topped any adult resident's list of grievances. It was just that black folks' presence in public spaces was where they encountered white supremacy with a raw, daily intensity. Moreover, nearly a decade of boycotts, sit-ins, and street demonstrations had now shown this side of the South's racial regime to be the most vulnerable. Consequently, during the ten weeks following the Birmingham settlement almost fifteen thousand people were arrested in 758 demonstrations in 186 cities across the nation.

The march on Washington

Given the Kennedy administration's earlier foot-dragging on civil rights legislation, A. Philip Randolph had been considering reviving a tactic he had used successfully against Roosevelt and Truman: the threat of a mass march on Washington focused on economic issues. In response to the Birmingham protests, President Kennedy had sent an omnibus civil rights bill to Congress that June, which raised the prospect of merging Randolph's march for jobs with SCLC's march in support of broader civil rights legislation. Jobs and voting rights had almost always been a part of the demands of local campaigns, but it had now become abundantly clear that the most effective way to achieve those goals required federal legislation and enforcement. Thus did the "March on Washington for Jobs and Freedom" come to be.

Therefore, even as scores of southern cities, influenced by Birmingham's example, launched protests at the local level, national civil rights groups coalesced around planning and preparing for a massive march on Washington similar to those implemented by white World War I bonus marchers in the 1920s and threatened by Randolph in the 1940s. To build national momentum, King undertook mass rallies in major population centers in the months preceding the march: from huge crowds in Cleveland he went on to address 50,000 in Los Angeles a week later and then 125,000 in Detroit on June 23. At the latter event, King delivered an early draft of the "I Have a Dream" speech (even earlier versions had appeared during the Birmingham campaign and in Savannah, Georgia). Later that summer it would emerge as the iconic expression of the faith and hopes of the early Civil Rights Movement.

Given their growing commitment to mobilizing ordinary people to realize their own power to effect enduring change as opposed to simply staging dramatic national events, many members of SNCC's staff were skeptical of both the wisdom of the proposed march and the efficacy of the civil rights bill it was intended to support. Field workers in local communities had been struggling to mobilize an aroused black populace to brave economic retaliation and outright murder to force local authorities to change. By contrast, the proposed march on Washington would be a demonstration aimed at mobilizing outside forces—the federal government and sympathetic white voters in the North—to adopt laws mandating that change. Moreover, the original plans advanced by some militants to bring the civil disobedience campaign to the streets of the nation's capital were abandoned, leaving only what was in essence a petition campaign to an ostensibly sympathetic government and the nation's citizenry. But this strategy was premised on the idea that one was indeed addressing a potential ally rather than a deeply ambivalent one in the office of the president or even a hostile one at the headquarters of the FBI, where J. Edgar Hoover was intent on discrediting rather than protecting southern civil rights activists.

The differences in perspective soon emerged in the march organizers' mandates regarding approved placards and general messaging, which strictly prohibited slogans that might give offense. Marchers obediently adhered to the agreed-on timing and duration of the march itself: in town after sunrise and out by sunset. For many veteran protesters who had endured beatings and abuse, this stress on decorum was grating. The different agendas and orientations of the march organizers broke into open conflict when Archbishop Patrick O'Boyle objected to the militant

The Civil Rights Movement

speech SNCC chairman John Lewis proposed to deliver, which contrary to Movement practice had to be preapproved. Likening the southern campaigns to Sherman's march through Georgia proved too much for the prelate and many others among march leaders. Other defects of the march organization could not as easily be blamed on recently added supporters, however. The official program for the main event at the Lincoln Memorial offered no opportunity for any of the Movement's black women activists to address the crowd that day. That shameful decision—or oversight—was all too consistent for a male leadership that had pushed Movement veterans like Ella Baker, Septima Clark, and others to the veiled corners of its history.

These deficiencies notwithstanding, the march was almost universally hailed as a great success. Having pushed the civil rights agenda to the center of international as well as national attention, it undoubtedly did lend momentum to congressional action. There was no viable second act to follow up on the march, however, which meant that once again the agenda shifted from direct action in southern streets to lobbying and deal making in the nation's capital, the NAACP's well-honed, chosen turf. Those efforts were certain to be confronted by an equally well-honed and powerfully entrenched southern congressional delegation that had thwarted and deflected earlier racial reform initiatives. Thus, the fate of this new effort would ultimately turn on extraneous and unanticipated events.

The slaughter of innocents

Except for the mob violence visited on the Freedom Riders, southern white resistance to the movement had been kept largely in the hands of legally constituted, political authorities since Emmett Till's murder. And except for "Bull" Connor's lapse in judgment during the Children's March in Birmingham, police violence or tolerance of mob violence had not been sufficient to discredit the white South's resistance to change. After the

Birmingham settlement and a summer of widespread protests, however, the secretive vigilante forces that had long policed the southern racial order began to reemerge. Just a day after the settlement was announced in Birmingham, a bomb ripped through a motel owned by A. G. Gaston followed shortly after by another that demolished the home of A. D. King, Martin's younger brother. Birmingham's NAACP leader Arthur Shores would endure a similar assault in September. Although no one was physically injured in this initial wave of terrorism, the nonviolence ethic was sorely tested as King and James Bevel tried to calm an angry black community.

Just a month later, however, Medgar Evers, whose demands for Birmingham-style concessions in Jackson, Mississippi, had made him a Klan target, was shot down in his driveway in the early morning hours of June 12, 1963. Evers's murder occurred just hours after President Kennedy had spoken to the nation promising his administration's support for an omnibus civil rights law. The signs were clear, however, that each step forward in black America's quest for human dignity would be met with a murderous response.

The most heinous—and arguably consequential—came at 10:22 on a Sunday morning, just eighteen days after the March on Washington had held out the hope for national reform. At that moment, fifteen sticks of dynamite attached to a timing device demolished the east side of Birmingham's Sixteenth Street Baptist Church, the principal staging ground for the demonstrations launched five months earlier. Four young girls attending Sunday School that day—three fourteen-year-olds, Addie Mae Collins, Carole Robertson, and Cynthia Wesley, and eleven-year-old Carol Denise McNair—were killed.

Thus, a Movement launched in no small measure in response to the murder of a teenaged boy in the Mississippi Delta was confronted with yet another wanton slaughter of innocents. Whatever optimism the summer's campaigns and national march had generated was deflated. An ostensibly New South city had turned its other face to the nation, one that echoed the terrorist campaigns of another time and place. In its aftermath—reinforced by future atrocities—the focus and temper of the Movement would change. For many veterans of earlier struggles, their faith in the nation's capacity to respond adequately to demonstrations of injustice faltered. The recalcitrance of a reemerging Old South would deepen that skepticism.

The violent assault on innocent black life at the Sixteenth Street Church was followed two months later by the assassination of President Kennedy, an event that raised further doubts about the fate of the proposed civil rights bill, now in the hands of a southern-born president who as Senate majority leader had facilitated the passage of compromised and only marginally effective civil rights laws in 1957 and 1960. By year's end, the previous summer's March on Washington seemed but a fleeting moment of hope—almost an interlude—in a year otherwise marked by intense racial violence.

Shortly after Kennedy's assassination, SNCC leaders gathered in Washington to discuss plans for an expanded voter registration project in Mississippi the following summer. For most of them nonviolence was increasingly a tactical choice rather than a moral commitment. Although there were SNCC and CORE members who were firmly committed to nonviolence as a way of life, this was not a philosophy embraced by most of the people they sought to lead. During his maiden trip to Mississippi, Bob Moses had felt uncomfortable in the home of his well-armed host. A few years later, SNCC and CORE offices were routinely protected by local black men armed with shotguns. They had become painfully aware that the relative restraints imposed by the aspirations of New South cities no longer applied. As these battle-hardened organizers readied themselves to pursue the freedom struggle into uncharted waters, they discovered that Mississippi was, to echo the title of James Baldwin's recently published novel, "another country."

Chapter 4

Organizing in the "American Congo": Mississippi's Freedom Summer and its aftermath

There is a striking irony about the chronology and character of the so-called classic Civil Rights Movement: Many of its participants attribute their own commitments to it, if not its very origins, to the brutal murder of Emmett Till, and yet the major mobilizations during its first decade emerged far beyond the site of Till's martyrdom. The casual brutality of a teenage boy's murder and mutilation of his body compounded by the bland indifference of white Mississippians to punishing the crime, made clear that this state was not a favorable place to mobilize a mass movement. In retrospect, it is equally clear that the grievances that sparked equal rights mobilizations elsewhere in the South were largely irrelevant to the lives and injustices suffered by most black Mississippians, then or later. Even for blacks from other southern states, Mississippi seemed a place out of time, a good place "to be from" went a wry and bitter joke. Or, as William Pickens, an NAACP staffer investigating a gruesome lynching in 1921, called it, "the American Congo." Written at a moment when King Leopold's reign of unconscionable terror in the Belgian Congo was being widely condemned—even by other colonial powers—as marking the outer boundaries of human depravity, Pickens's depiction was damning indeed.

Pickens's characterization referred to the Delta, the corridor framed by the counties stretching along both sides of the

Mississippi River from southeastern Missouri down to Vicksburg, which was one of the most fertile cotton regions in the South. This region was less a remnant of its antebellum slave empire than an early twentieth-century creation of northern and English capitalists that would come to be known later for its extreme poverty and racial terror. In the 1890s, it had been a refuge for black migrants seeking independent farms free from the oppressive conditions of the old cotton economy of the southeastern states. In the Delta they could cut timber for good wages and buy land. At the dawn of the twentieth century, descendants of these pioneers still accounted for two out of every three farm owners in the region, but a quarter-century later most of them had been reduced to landless laborers on vast industrial plantations—literally totalitarian communities that supplied them bare subsistence, monitored their mail, and restrained their every movement.

As elsewhere in the South, however, white hegemony in the Delta began to erode under the pressure of social and economic changes set in motion during the First World War and the Great Migration. The interwar period witnessed flickers of resistance as farmers' unions and chapters of both the NAACP and Marcus Garvey's United Negro Improvement Association became active. In the aftermath of the Second World War, those flickers flamed even brighter and bolder as returning veterans mounted more militant and visible challenges to the racial order. Notable among the activists undertaking these initiatives were veterans of the recent world war, men like Amzie Moore, Aaron Henry, and Medgar Evers. A postal worker before the war, Moore became a community leader and relatively successful businessman in Bolivar County. Henry studied pharmacology at Xavier University in New Orleans after his service in the Pacific before returning home in 1950 to Clarksdale, Coahoma County's principal city, where he became a pharmacist and eventually purchased a drugstore.

Meanwhile, Evers, who had seen combat during the Normandy invasion, returned home determined to get a college degree and the ballot. Two days before the Fourth of July holiday in 1946, he led a group of fellow veterans to the registrar's office in Decatur, Mississippi. After being violently rebuffed during two attempts to register, he gave up on the vote for a while but was able to graduate from Alcorn State College with a business degree. After graduation he moved to Mound Bayou in the Mississippi Delta to work as an insurance agent for Dr. Theodore Roosevelt Mason Howard, an entrepreneur and early civil rights activist in the state. In 1951, Evers, Moore, and Henry joined Dr. Howard to establish the Regional Council of Negro Leadership and launched an unsuccessful boycott of segregated gas station restrooms. They also undertook a voter registration campaign, however, that contributed substantially to the twenty-two thousand new black voters added to the state's voter rolls by the early 1950s. In 1954, almost a decade before James Meredith entered the University of Mississippi under federal guard, Evers had taken the bold, though unsuccessful, step of attempting to enroll in its law school.

When civil rights organizers arrived in the early 1960s, therefore, they found not a blank slate but communities imbued with histories of struggle and an experienced core of indigenous black leaders ready to mentor the outsiders and show them where to start. Unlike other southern states, ministers had not taken leading roles in civil rights activism in Mississippi. Its activists were more likely to resemble Evers, Moore, Henry, and Howard: small to medium-sized entrepreneurs enjoying a measure of independence from the direct, immediate control of white powers. In the Delta and elsewhere in the state, business proprietors like Vera Pigee, a beautician in Clarksdale, and farm owners like E. W. Steptoe and Herbert Lee in Amity and Lamar Smith in Lincoln led the way. The eventual martyrdom of Lee and Smith underscores the harsh reality that such courageous people were not invulnerable to the violence then endemic to Mississippi, or to economic pressures from bankers, suppliers, and licensing authorities. They were, nonetheless, much less vulnerable than most rural Mississippians laboring on plantations under the direct surveillance of employer-landlords, and thus certain to lose both their shelter and their job at the first sign of their challenging the social order.

The fate of Fannie Lou Hamer reveals the harsh retaliation that awaited the slightest sign of resistance by the state's plantation workers. Since early childhood Hamer had worked the cotton of W. D. Marlowe's plantation near Ruleville for less than four dollars a day, along with her parents and nineteen siblings. In contrast to many of her peers, Fannie Lou's elementary schooling had left her just literate enough to read the Bible and secure a promotion to plantation timekeeper in 1944, about the time she married her husband, "Pap," who drove a tractor there. Hamer had also attended at least one of the annual meetings of Dr. Howard's RCNL. That experience may have predisposed her in August 1962 to join a group SNCC recruited to undertake the thirty-mile journey to Sunflower's county seat in Indianola to register to vote. It was not surprising that she failed the so-called literacy test requiring her to answer an obscure point of law, but it *was* surprising that news of her attempt to register reached the Marlowe plantation boss well before she got home that evening. Presented the choice of either withdrawing her registration application or leaving the plantation that very night, Hamer chose the latter. This was merely the beginning of a sustained campaign of violent intimidation that she and other applicants endured over the coming months, as Klansmen regularly fired into the homes of anyone who gave them shelter, and police harassment was commonplace.

Hamer's story reflects the obstacles the Movement faced in mobilizing resistance among a laboring population, which, though rapidly diminishing, was still enmeshed in the carceral regime of the plantation economy. It also underscores the prominence of women among those who led the nascent resistance to that regime. Six months after her eviction from the Marlowe plantation, Hamer managed to pass the literacy test and registered to vote. She owed that success to the tutelage of Annell Ponder, who was herself a graduate of Septima Clark's literacy program. A native of Atlanta and graduate of Clark College, Ponder had been recruited to run a citizenship workshop in Greenwood, Mississippi, as her first assignment with SCLC. Returning from South Carolina after a voter registration workshop in June 1963, Ponder, Hamer, and several other women in the group were viciously beaten by the arresting officer and the jailers in Winona, Mississippi. Nonetheless, the women, including two teenagers—fifteen-year-old June Johnson and seventeen-year-old Euvester Simpson—would all go on to redouble their commitments to the Mississippi Movement in the months and years to come.

The biographies of other prominent female activists in the Mississippi Movement were in some ways similar to those of indigenous male leaders like Evers and Henry in that they had also benefited from opportunities that the war and postwar developments provided. Although born in Mobile, Alabama, in 1912, Annie Bell Robinson Devine was raised in Canton, Mississippi. She had attended Tougaloo College, and like Evers worked as an insurance agent after graduation, and then taught school before joining the CORE staff in the Delta. Born in 1926 and raised in Hattiesburg, where her grandparents owned a farm, Victoria Gray Adams managed to attend Wilberforce University in Ohio for one year before marrying a soldier, who was stationed first in Germany and then in Maryland. After divorcing him, she returned to Hattiesburg, Mississippi, where she did voter education and became a full-time field worker with SNCC. For Gray Adams, the Movement was "what I'd been looking for all of my conscious existence. . . . It was like coming home." In 1964, Gray Adams would run to represent Mississippi in the US Senate.

In many ways, then, the character of the Mississippi Movement differed from the campaigns that had preceded it. The small towns and rural outposts of Mississippi offered a very different terrain of struggle than New South cities, one demanding different organizing strategies, tactics, and goals. Contesting access to public accommodations was largely irrelevant in the rural areas of Deep South states like Mississippi and Alabama, where public accommodations were largely absent, or relatively primitive at best. With an annual median income ranging from a low of $819 in Quitman to a high of $1,600 in Washington County, leaving fully three-quarters of its population below the 1960 national poverty line, the Delta was a particularly poor target for consumer-oriented protests. Relatively isolated as well as impoverished, such communities were also much less conducive to the boycotts, sit-ins, and mass street demonstrations that had rocked New South cities for almost a decade. Nonviolent confrontations with police, moreover, were likely to be both fruitless and dangerous, given the difficulty in attracting sustained media attention to restrain local authorities and to pressure them or national elites into negotiations and possible concessions. Moreover, nonviolent direct action could be suicidal in jurisdictions where protesters could be killed in full view of witnesses without fear of legal repercussions.

On the other hand, Mississippi, along with much of the rest of the rural Deep South, remained an obvious target for campaigns to increase black voter registration. Even though most of the black voters registered in the early postwar years had been summarily purged from the state's rolls by the mid-1950s, the potential for a black political revolution remained clear. This was especially evident in the Delta, where blacks accounted for 64 percent of the population in 1960. In fact, only five of its eighteen counties had a black population below 60 percent. Thus, when Bob Moses's recruiting trip for SNCC brought him to Amzie Moore's door in the summer of 1960, Moore told him that the best thing SNCC could do for Mississippi was to send volunteers to help with voter registration. It turned out that Moore was no more ready to make use of such volunteers at that moment than Moses or SNCC was prepared to send them. When SNCC finally did respond to Moore's request the following year, however, it had become clear that it would require a radical change in its agenda and, indeed, in the character of the Movement as a whole.

A new organizing agenda

After their second meeting, in the summer of 1961, Moses followed up Moore's suggestion that he contact C. C. Bryant, the president of the NAACP chapter in McComb, a town in Pike County, near the Louisiana border and roughly eighty miles south of the state capital at Jackson. Thus, Moses's first major effort to register Mississippi voters began far from the Delta region that would later become the focus of SNCC's Mississippi campaign and, ironically, in a region bearing place names like Lincoln and Lamar, which reflected its history in the past century when it was a hotbed of black Reconstruction politics. Moses began organizing a wary and vulnerable people by spending weeks simply listening to them. Only then did he try to prepare them to enter alienating courthouses and sheriff's offices where they would confront confusing literacy tests administered by hostile registrars. After some encouraging initial successes, white resistance stiffened and violence erupted as the tempo of registration attempts quickened. In Liberty, Amite's ironically misnamed county seat, Moses was arrested and jailed while accompanying aspiring voters to the registrar's office. Shortly afterward he was assaulted by the sheriff's cousin and needed eight stitches to close a head wound. The local court found the sheriff's cousin not guilty.

Although his effort was eventually reinforced by the arrival of a dozen more SNCC workers, Moses's focus on canvassing voters was soon overtaken by the very different ambitions of the area's high school youth, who were determined to emulate the daring challenges to segregated lunch counters they had witnessed elsewhere. Much like Charles Sherrod and Cordell Reagon in Albany, therefore, the SNCC field workers found themselves drawn into supporting sit-ins that these young people launched at Woolworth's and the Greyhound bus station. This and similar developments in Jackson delayed further progress in the registration campaign, especially when many of the students were expelled from school, which, in contrast with earlier campaigns, turned many of the parents against the Freedom Riders. The brutal murder in broad daylight of Herbert Lee by a state legislator eroded the community's support even further, effectively shutting down the project after just four months.

The growing body count made clear that organizing the rural Deep South was a life-and-death decision. How people—ordinary people—came to make that decision was not a question to be taken lightly. This campaign would require different strategies and means of protecting both organizers and participants. The nonviolent discipline necessary during sit-ins and street demonstrations was useless in situations in which violent attacks came from nightriders and assassins. Confronting such terrorism, local black communities eventually turned to armed self-defense to protect the activists as best they could.

It was against this backdrop that the SNCC field staff had gathered at the Highlander center in August 1961 for a tense three-day debate over the future direction of their movement. The initial question was whether SNCC should shift its resources into voter registration projects, which many feared meant abandoning the direct-action campaigns that had defined the organization from its inception. But lurking within that contentious question was another, even more troubling one: How to pursue the new agenda in regions where experience had shown that black lives did not matter to either local white authorities or their national counterparts?

On the other hand, dramatic scenes of violence like that inflicted on the Freedom Riders had exposed the Kennedy administration's lack of control of the situation, and that did matter. Indeed, it mattered enough to prod Justice Department officials into brokering meetings during the summer of 1961 between representatives of the major civil rights organizations and several private foundations known to have previously supported liberal legal and labor activism. The government was motivated by a transparent effort to shift Movement activities from confrontational direct-action campaigns into voter registration, which they mistakenly assumed would attract less violent white opposition.

Although fully aware of this, the civil rights groups saw an opportunity in these deliberations for attracting badly needed organizational support for increasing the number of black voters, a goal that had been part of the equal rights agenda since the past century. Although some SNCC field staff were already engaged in voter registration projects in McComb and Albany, the Highlander debate appeared doomed to stalemate until Ella Baker suggested the obvious solution: Do both direct action and voter registration. No doubt Jim Forman and others in the central office were aware as well that funding from the Voter Education Project (VEP) would help SNCC's bottom line, especially since staffers could be transferred from one task to another as the situation dictated.

Nonetheless, SNCC's debate over tactics and strategy had exposed fundamental questions about the future of the Movement in the rural Deep South. As Bob Moses had already discovered in McComb, voter mobilization in a terrorist state required a different approach to community organizing. Successful and enduring organizing required that strong personal bonds be forged with and among a vulnerable people. Only in this way could an organic, indigenous leadership emerge from these communities able to endure the ups and downs that any project was bound to face. The emphasis had to be on listening rather than preaching, which not only established trust but was also the way one learned the personal histories that often revealed a people's already existing capacities for resistance. It helped, therefore, that most of the initial corps of SNCC workers were Mississippi natives steeped in its cultural idioms and language. The principal audience for Movement actions would not be found in faraway capitals but within the community itself. Thus, while mass meetings in churches continued to be important for this work, one also had to reach out to people wherever they might be found and preferably in places relatively secure from white surveillance—in barbershops, beauty parlors, and pool halls, as well as through the multitude of other social networks that grounded any community. All in all, this was the kind of fieldwork Ella Baker had been urging during her tenures with the NAACP and SCLC and finally with the young folk in SNCC. Ironically, it was a lesson only half-learned by SNCC folk as well. It was in truth a strategy that yielded disappointingly few new black voters in the summer of 1963, certainly, but it would ultimately shake the foundations of the South's racial order.

A critical part of the proposed VEP agreement was that the Justice Department promised to take action to protect workers who were obstructed by local authorities or threatened with violence. It soon became clear, however, that despite its vocal support of equal rights, the Kennedy administration was fatally compromised by its political reliance on the powerful southern wing of the Democratic congressional delegation, which could block its entire legislative agenda. Thus, while registration efforts proceeded fairly smoothly in the Upper South, they were thwarted in the Deep South by both legal obstruction and vigilante violence. By late summer 1963, the Council of Federated Organizations (COFO), which had been organized to coordinate the VEP project in Mississippi, began planning for a more aggressive and broader attack on blacks' disenfranchisement. It would push the voter registration campaign into more Mississippi counties and stage a mock election that fall as a tactic both to educate blacks politically and to demonstrate to the nation their desire for the ballot. Since this ambitious project required far more canvassers than COFO could

8. Two black men in Hattiesburg, Mississippi, fill out voter registration forms on January 22, 1964, at the Forest County Courthouse office while registrar Therand Lind (standing on the left) supervises. The sign on the wall above them was typical of the intimidation tactics of local officials to discourage black applicants from registering.

supply, it recruited students from Yale and Stanford to buttress the workforce.

The fact that eighty-three thousand people cast "freedom ballots" that November was considered a great victory, despite the low turnout in some of the counties where blacks were most vulnerable to violence. Sandwiched between the Birmingham bombing in September and the assassination of President Kennedy in November, COFO's unprecedented achievement received very little notice beyond the activists involved. Nonetheless, planning began almost immediately for an even more ambitious campaign the following summer, one aimed at not only increased voter registration but also the election of delegates who would challenge the seating of the state's delegation at the Democratic National Convention in Atlantic City that August. By offering a biracial slate of candidates chosen in a free and open election, the proposed Mississippi Freedom Democratic Party (MFDP) would expose the blatant racial discrimination of the putatively "regular" Democrats.

Freedom Summer

As COFO leaders began planning for the summer project of registering and canvassing voters for the MFDP's challenge at the national party's convention in Atlantic City, it became clear that a far larger field staff was required. Building on the previous year's experience, recruiting northern college students to assist with the freedom ballot seemed a logical solution. Although a number of SNCC veterans opposed the idea, fearing an inevitable change in the character and elan of the Movement, Bob Moses and Fannie Lou Hamer made strong arguments in support. It is likely that his bloody experience in McComb had convinced Moses that the project was doomed to fail without federal protection. And it was becoming painfully clear that only the powerful social connections of the families of white students from elite colleges would ensure such protection.

The test of that theory came quickly. In mid-June, 250 of the 650 students who volunteered to work for the "freedom vote" in Mississippi that summer gathered for two weeks of orientation and training at the Western College for Women in Oxford, Ohio. Although the training sessions attempted to convey some sense of the challenges to come, nothing could prepare the tutees for the terror awaiting them.

Before they even reached their assigned destinations, they learned that one of the summer volunteers, Andrew Goodman, and two more experienced CORE organizers—Michael ("Mickey") Schwerner and James Chaney—had gone missing. All three men were in their early twenties. Goodman and Schwerner were white,

Jewish college students from New York; Chaney was a black native of Meridian, Mississippi, who had become active the previous fall during the Freedom Ballot campaign in Canton and gone on to organize a freedom school in Greenwood. Schwerner's activism had begun earlier that year when he and his wife, Rita, joined CORE. Just three months later, Schwerner found himself in charge of the eastern section of Mississippi's fourth congressional district, which COFO had assigned to CORE. Despite their limited experience, the Schwerners made rapid progress in gaining the confidence and support of local blacks, who helped them set up a community center and allowed them to use Mount Zion Methodist Church for a freedom school. Local whites retaliated by burning down the church, among the first of the thirty-five arson attacks on black churches that summer.

Feeling an urgent need to provide support and reassurance to the devastated congregation, the three left Oxford to investigate the incident, but were arrested in Philadelphia, Neshoba's county seat, ostensibly for a traffic violation. Since the three men were released later that night, the arrest was likely a ruse to provide time to mobilize the local Klan and provide them a description of Schwerner's car, which the State Sovereignty Commission had helpfully circulated earlier. Shortly after their release they were stopped again by Deputy Cecil Price, but this time to be turned over to waiting Klansmen.

Given the media attention focused on Oxford and the continuing coverage of the white student volunteers who had arrived in Mississippi, the story of the three men's disappearance became national news. Unlike earlier murders, these would not be ignored. President Johnson sent Central Intelligence Agency (CIA) director Allen Dulles to the state, followed in short order by Federal Bureau of Investigation (FBI) director J. Edgar Hoover. Although these visits amounted to little more than photo ops, they did keep the possibility of foul play on the nation's front pages. Meanwhile, searchers for the three missing men turned up other unpublicized murder victims in the waterways and swamps of the state, further exposing its callous disregard of racial violence against black Mississippians.

Two days before Schwerner, Chaney, and Goodman disappeared, Congress passed legislation barring discrimination in public accommodations and employment, but the discovery of their bodies under an earthen dam forty-six days later soured the sense of victory. Nothing in the new civil rights law secured black voting rights in jurisdictions ruled by terrorists.

Freedom schools and the Mississippi challenge

Although the tragic deaths of the three civil rights workers were a demoralizing blow, they did not deter the volunteers' commitment to the larger cause or the innovations they pursued. The voter registration campaign that emerged in Mississippi's Freedom Summer would be very different from other VEP projects elsewhere in the South. Committed to the task of sparking deeper and more lasting change in these long-oppressed communities, SNCC and CORE staffers pursued new organizing techniques to address the profound problems they encountered. Since the pioneering work of Septima Clark in South Carolina, voter registration campaigns had been grounded in patiently tutoring eligible adults in the basic literacy skills and civic knowledge necessary to pass registration tests expressly designed to exclude black voters. As civil rights organizers embedded themselves in Mississippi's black communities, however, they uncovered more profound disabilities that would complicate the task of mobilizing them. Ironically, the local students' activism exposed these problems. When more than a hundred students in McComb were expelled for participating in civil rights demonstrations in 1961, SNCC workers there had opened "Nonviolent High" to provide an alternative space for instruction. A year later, local staff in Greenwood started an impromptu after-school program for the students who regularly gathered in their offices. These improvised initiatives soon exposed how desperately the state school system was shortchanging black students. In Bolivar County, for example, the school board not only forbade instruction in foreign languages or civics but also excluded the Reconstruction period from US history courses entirely.

Drawing on these experiences, a SNCC field staffer, Charlie Cobb, proposed in the fall of 1963 that COFO broaden its voter education project to include compensatory education, or "freedom schools." With curricular advice from history professors Staughton Lynd and Howard Zinn, both of whom were teaching at that time at Spelman, a black women's college in Atlanta, an ambitious cultural enrichment and political education program became part of the larger summer project. Thus did Cobb's freedom school idea blossom in the summer of 1964, when, drawing on the additional help of its volunteers, SNCC opened fifty-five freedom schools serving 2,500 students, including some adults. In time the ideas tested in this project would reappear in diverse educational settings across the nation, including federally funded poverty programs and the independent community schools opened by northern black nationalists later that decade.

The overt political work of Freedom Summer was not deflected by the violence that had marred its initiation either. Step by step, COFO's political insurgency built the case against the state's regular Democratic Party. Deprived of voting rights in the regular Democratic primary, COFO held its own convention a month after the passage of the Civil Rights Act in July. Those delegates convened on August 6, pointedly in the same church in Jackson where Medgar Evers's funeral had been held the previous summer. They elected a biracial delegation to represent the party at the national convention scheduled to open in Atlantic City later that month. Making careful preparations for that meeting, the MFDP succeeded in securing the support of nine of the eleven state delegations on the Credentials Committee that it would need to bring its case to the floor of the convention.

But much as the Kennedys had feared the entrenched southern congressional delegation's hostility to their legislative agenda, Lyndon Johnson feared a convention walkout that might imperil his election that fall. Just weeks after securing the passage of the Civil Rights Act, therefore, Johnson threw the full weight of his presidential powers to defeat the MFDP challengers. Thus did the president of the United States marshal strong-arm tactics—such as withdrawing offers of judgeships and government jobs, and even canceling bank loans—to force delegates to recant support they had previously offered the insurgents' cause. Meanwhile, indirect pressure was brought to bear on prominent liberals and erstwhile civil rights champions—including soon-to-be vice president Hubert Humphrey and the heads of the major labor unions—to pressure the MFDP supporters to compromise. Despite the powerful, nationally televised testimony of Fannie Lou Hamer before the Credentials Committee, the president's opposition succeeded in defeating the challenge, even though it still provoked many of the regular southern delegates to walk out.

In retrospect, Stokely Carmichael's subsequent assessment that this was, in fact, "the flat-out dumbest political miscalculation [the] Democratic Party leadership ever made" has merit. The decision badly fractured the civil rights alliance, leaving in its wake distrust and suspicions that would not soon—if ever—be entirely dispelled. While the NAACP played its predictable role of siding with the party establishment, other more radical allies, such as Bayard Rustin, were also critical of the insurgents' refusal to compromise. Of the major civil rights leaders, only Martin Luther King Jr. stood firm with the MFDP.

For people who had endured a brutal summer of bloodshed and violence, the disillusionment was profound and lasting. As John

Lewis, one of the more moderate voices among the SNCC leadership, observed:

> Until then, despite every setback and disappointment and obstacle
> we had faced over the years, the belief still prevailed that the system
> would work, the system would listen, the system would respond.
> Now, for the first time, we had made our way to the very center of
> the system. We had played by the rules, done everything we were
> supposed to do, had played the game exactly as required, had
> arrived at the doorstep and found the door slammed in our face.

Or, as Bob Moses told the delegation, expressing what had until then been the core theme of Movement philosophy: "We're not here to bring politics to our morality, but to bring morality to our politics."

Both Lewis and Moses would soon retire from SNCC as it began to change course yet again. The lesson for many of the veterans who remained was that the core objective of their struggle was not about achieving a more just morality but the justice of a more equitable distribution of political power. Although the eventual articulation of that vision would cause consternation among former allies as well as enemies, it was arguably the logical conclusion of a project focused on securing the legitimate political rights of a disfranchised community.

Selma

Roughly six months after the "Mississippi Challenge" was defeated in Atlantic City, the issue of voting rights—and the inequitable distribution of political power that lay at the heart of that challenge—took center stage in the civil rights struggle. A voter registration campaign centered on the small town of Selma and its surrounding counties had been initiated at roughly the same time as COFO began organizing in the Mississippi Delta. Unlike the Challenge, however, the Alabama campaign would mark the final, unambiguous triumph of one of the principal goals of the "classic"

Civil Rights Movement, even as the terrain and character of the larger freedom struggle would change fundamentally in its aftermath. Indeed, in many ways the victory at Selma masked those changes in organizational and movement dynamics, most of which had been under way since the defeat in Atlantic City.

Nonetheless, the tactics and strategies that would produce victory in Selma were much the same as those deployed in New South cities over the preceding decade: Expose the brutal injustice of the Jim Crow system to a horrified national public that would press the federal government to act. Fittingly, perhaps, Selma and its rural hinterland were a microcosm of New South and Old, and thus well suited to that strategy. On road maps Selma is more than twice as far from Philadelphia, Mississippi, which is near the site of one of the Movement's most infamous atrocities, than it is from Montgomery, the modern Movement's birthplace. By 1965, however, it was in many ways much closer to the former in its social character. In contrast with the New South cities where mass demonstrations had been most effective, Selma's 1960s population of 28,385 more closely resembled some of the principal sites of activism in the Mississippi Delta: places like Greenwood, with 20,436 residents, or Clarksdale with 21,105, or, at the upper end, Hattiesburg with 34,989. The fact that almost half its residents were black matched the demographic profile of many other small towns in the rural Deep South.

And, yet, one could also find political dynamics and economic trends there similar to those in New South cities like Montgomery and Birmingham. Fifty years earlier Dallas County had lost the status it had held for more than half a century as the state's premier cotton producer and had begun a transformation similar to much of the rest of the South, spurred by the structural changes wrought by two world wars and a vast out-migration of its population. By 1964, only one thousand black tenant farmers were left of the seven thousand in the county in 1910. Cattle ranches had gradually replaced cotton plantations, and repurposed transportation networks brought in urban jobs and unions. As in Albany, the Second World War added a military installation to the mix, when Craig Air Force Base was established to train fighter pilots. As in New South cities, too, these structural changes produced tensions among the white political elite, pitting a reputedly "progressive" group seeking urban business expansion and outside investment against the more reactionary forces that controlled the county administration. In a political scenario similar to Montgomery's a decade earlier, and despite their much smaller numbers, black voters provided the margin of victory to elect a racial "moderate," Joseph Smitherman, to the mayor's office. Along with police chief Wilson Baker, Smitherman tried to cultivate—with diminishing success—his reputation as a racial moderate. Tellingly, however, this would bring Baker, whose "moderation" resembled the calculated approach to law enforcement of Albany's Laurie Pritchett, into frequent conflict with Dallas County sheriff Jim Clark, whose methods emulated the brutal practices of Birmingham's "Bull" Connor, who just happened to be a native of the county.

Months before the Mississippi campaign hit its stride, Bernard Lafayette, a veteran organizer who had worked with both SCLC and SNCC, and his wife, Colia, who had worked with the NAACP's Medgar Evers, joined SNCC veteran Worth Long to begin organizing a voter registration campaign in Selma. Shortly after the Sixteenth Street Church bombing in September 1963, Diane Nash and James Bevel, despite previously being among the firmest advocates of direct action, had also urged SCLC to commit to a voter registration campaign in Selma as a fitting response to that atrocity. Thus, both SNCC and SCLC were at least nominally committed to Selma well before the Mississippi Challenge faltered in Atlantic City the following year. Despite the initial enthusiasm and some spirited nightly mass meetings, however, progress had been uneven, and by the fall of 1964 the project had stalled in the face of intense economic pressures on eligible voters and local leaders. This led one of the local leaders, Amelia Boynton, to appeal for King's direct involvement, to which King assented. He returned the following January, after receiving the Nobel Peace Prize in December, which ensured the national attention Boynton had sought.

Within weeks the mobilization accelerated to a crisis as large groups, sometimes numbering in the thousands, marched to registration sites. Predictably, Sheriff Clark responded with violence, which encouraged attacks by vigilante groups as well. Following a nighttime demonstration, rioting police clubbed Jimmie Lee Jackson to death while he tried to shield his mother from their blows. Responding to Jackson's martyrdom, SCLC organized a march to Montgomery to lay its grievances before the state government. The marchers, led by SNCC chairman John Lewis, were only able to reach the bridge separating the town of Selma from the county, however: There Sheriff Clark's posse clubbed them into submission and retreat. That event, witnessed by a national television audience, would later be memorialized as "Bloody Sunday." Sympathy demonstrations erupted in cities across the nation, and around-the-clock pickets enveloped the White House. As in Birmingham, King issued a plea for national support that brought hundreds of sympathizers to Selma to join the campaign. Almost immediately, one of them, James Reeb, a Unitarian minister from Boston, was killed by vigilantes. Facing a national crisis threatening to spin out of control, the federal district court granted the demonstrators permission to proceed with a planned march from Selma to the state capital in Montgomery, and under that authority President Johnson ordered federal protection for the more than three thousand marchers who undertook the fifty-four-mile journey. Johnson also made a dramatic address to the nation announcing support for a voting rights bill that would address the marchers' grievances. Five months later, on August 6, he would sign the Voting Rights Act into law.

Selma would be the last sustained, community-wide mobilization in the South of a size, character, and style comparable to those

9. On Sunday, March 7, 1965, Dallas County sheriff's deputies attacked peaceful demonstrators on the Edmund Pettus Bridge in Selma, Alabama, as they began a march protesting voter discrimination. The event became known as "Bloody Sunday."

that had rocked the nation over the past decade. This is not to say that street protests ceased, but simply that those protests would not resemble Montgomery, Birmingham, or Albany in their size, the character of the broader black community's engagement, or in the strategy for change that informed them. The voting rights struggle had opened—or rather reopened—the conventional political process as a viable stage for movement activity. And this would be true in the North and West as well as the South.

Black power in Lowndes County

As marchers departed Montgomery, one of their number, a Detroit housewife and volunteer, Viola Liuzzo, was murdered while ferrying departing demonstrators to their destinations. Liuzzo's death underscored the terrible human cost of the political victory at Selma. It also, ironically, brought attention to Lowndes County, where the attack took place. It was there that SNCC would focus its attention as it tested its evolving paradigm for the Movement's future course. In the view of many SNCC veterans, Atlantic City had exposed a critical flaw in Movement philosophy, made even more manifest for some of those who took the tour of recently independent west African nations that Harry Belafonte funded afterward. In their view, appealing to a fickle northern public to pressure a fractured, often duplicitous federal bureaucracy was an unreliable strategy for effecting fundamental social change. The failure of the Challenge, one could argue, showed that it was not persuasion but power that offered the key to achieving meaningful change. Rural, black-majority counties like Lowndes offered an opportunity to demonstrate that truth, as well as to move on to the next phase of a freedom struggle that was increasingly national and international in scope.

"Enter Lowndes County and you back in the Mississippi Delta," was Stokely Carmichael's succinct description of the county. Certainly, the violence unleashed on voter registration workers in Lowndes was very similar to that encountered in Mississippi. Jonathan Daniels, a young Episcopal seminarian and volunteer, was shot down in broad daylight by Tom Coleman for seeking service at a country store. Like the killer of Herbert Lee in Amity three years earlier, Coleman would never be punished. In this lawless atmosphere SNCC workers sought protection, as they had in the Delta, by posting armed guards around their headquarters at night and constantly changing their residences to avoid being killed in their sleep.

And yet, like the Delta, Lowndes had also nurtured an indigenous leadership that was already at work on voting rights even before SNCC established a presence there. Earlier experiences with the Movement in Birmingham and Montgomery had shaped local activists John Hulett and Lillian McGill. Hulett had left his family's farm for Birmingham, where he worked with the local chapter of the NAACP and later with SCLC's Fred Shuttlesworth. McGill had lived in Montgomery, where she had participated in the bus boycott in 1955. Family crises brought both back to the county by the mid-1960s, and they each became involved in voter registration during the Selma crisis.

10. In March 1965 thousands of black and white protesters marched from Selma to Montgomery, Alabama, demanding an end to racial barriers to voting rights.

On March 19, two days before the Selma-to-Montgomery march began, Hulett convened the first meeting to organize a voter registration campaign in Lowndes. As in the Mississippi Delta, ministers were not a significant presence in the Lowndes County campaign, partly because most were itinerants who did not live there. As a consequence, churches were less likely to be sites for mobilization. Instead, various social clubs provided the network of contacts and meeting spaces for the initial organizational meetings. By late spring, with the help of Stokely Carmichael and other SNCC workers, a robust and expanded campaign brought hundreds of people to county registration sites. Later that fall, when the federal registrars authorized by the Voting Rights Act appeared to supervise the processing of applicants, those numbers soared even more. By the end of October, 40 percent of the county's eligible black voters had officially registered, and by year's end blacks made up almost half of the county's voters.

The registration campaign in Lowndes had been organized by the Lowndes County Freedom Organization, which in conformity with a state law requiring political parties to have an easily identifiable symbol chose the black panther for its logo. The panther symbol reflected the militant self-determination that had evolved in Lowndes and elsewhere in response to the perceived failures of the national Democratic Party to protect black life or the democratic process. As in Mississippi the previous year, this was an indigenous initiative, but one that SNCC under Carmichael's leadership fully embraced and publicized. Thus, the Lowndes County Panthers chose to run an independent slate of candidates for the midterm elections in 1966, a decision bitterly opposed by SCLC staffers such as Hosea Williams, who urged support of "moderate" white Democrats instead. Consequently, given a split black vote, the insurgents were defeated in this first test of a separatist black power strategy.

During the summer preceding those elections, however, Carmichael had seized an opportunity to cast a national spotlight on the strategy being field tested in Lowndes. When James Meredith, the maverick hero of the integration struggle at Ole Miss four years earlier, was shot during his one-man, so-called march against fear through the Mississippi Delta, most of the major civil rights organizations— except the NAACP—converged to complete the march. This attracted wall-to-wall media coverage, which Carmichael exploited to make "black power" the new mantra of the freedom struggle. Although the slogan contrasted sharply with the Gandhian ethos of nonviolent pressure and moral persuasion that had shaped the Movement since its inception, it would prove more resonant with the next stage of struggle in northern and western as well as southern cities.

Chapter 5
Freedom movements in the North

On July 23, 1963, just weeks before the March on Washington that August, Martin Luther King Jr. led a demonstration of 125,000 marchers down Detroit's Woodward Avenue, at the conclusion of which he delivered an early version of his "I Have A Dream" speech. At that time, this was the largest street demonstration he had ever led. Despite political and ideological differences among the mostly black demonstrators gathered to hear him, they were united on a common agenda demanding equality in schools and workplaces, and an end to police brutality. A month later, on the same day as the March on Washington, a sympathy demonstration in Seattle added housing discrimination to that list of grievances. Thus did these northern constituencies underscore issues that up to that point had had much less resonance in the southern movement.

The concurrence of these events underscores the complex interactions between the northern and southern wings of the Civil Rights Movement. Northern activism over the first five decades of the twentieth century had set the stage and provided the launch pad for the southern movements of the 1950s and 1960s, but the southern insurgencies had at least partly obscured the continuing struggles against northern racism. Indeed, to some extent many northern activists had been momentarily cast into largely supportive roles to the emerging southern freedom movement.

Northern support groups provided financial and material aid to Tennessee farmworkers evicted for seeking voting rights in 1959, picketed northern branches of stores targeted by southern sit-ins, and collected canned food and clothing to aid impoverished and embattled communities in Mississippi and elsewhere. Indeed, such initiatives were the first steps that drew some activists into the southern movement.

After Selma that trajectory would be reversed as veterans of the southern movement came north. What they confronted there were inequities that on the surface seemed the same as those found in the South—segregated schools, employment discrimination, and police brutality—but since most of them were not mandated by law, they posed somewhat different challenges regarding the most effective strategies and tactics to address them. Moreover, the timing of the renewed focus on black communities in the North and West occurred at the very moment black Americans in all regions of the country were becoming less receptive to nonviolent tactics and integrationist politics. It is arguable, therefore, that the revived movements in the North and West were a departure from, rather than an extension of, the southern Movement of the previous decade.

Schools

Although the *Brown v. Board of Education* decision triggered white southerners' massive resistance to racial justice, it is notable that Linda Brown, the lead plaintiff in that case, was protesting segregated schooling in Topeka, Kansas, a historic stronghold of abolitionism, rather than in a southern state. In fact, two of the other four cases bundled with Brown's were also from northern or border jurisdictions: *Gebhart v. Belton* from Delaware and *Bolling v. Sharpe* from the nation's capital. Notwithstanding the South's dismal failure to provide educational resources for black children, the schooling of northern black youth was also generally segregated and of poor quality by the third and fourth decades of the twentieth century, especially as the second wartime migration north exploded the demands on educational resources.

Consequently, in the same years that the Civil Rights Movement caught fire in scores of southern cities, there were school boycotts in Boston, New York City, and Chicago protesting inferior, segregated schools. School conditions for black youth in Chicago were especially egregious. The Chicago school board's adamant resistance to any integration measures had produced intolerable overcrowding, to which it responded by splitting the black schools' days into two foreshortened sessions and moving some classes into mobile trailers that black Chicagoans dubbed "Willis Wagons" (in satiric honor of the superintendent of schools, Benjamin Willis). Indeed, in the same month that the 1963 March on Washington was launched, SNCC and CORE demonstrators blocked construction crews from installing yet more "Willis Wagons." That demonstration was preceded by a CORE-sponsored, weeklong sit-in and hunger strike at the Board of Education offices, which was followed in October by a one-day boycott, a "Freedom Day," during which 225,000 student demonstrators chanted:

> What do we want?
> Books!
> When?
> Now!

These protests continued in concert with the more publicized events in the South. Thus, in June 1965, three months after the Selma-to-Montgomery march, 250 demonstrators were arrested for blocking traffic on Chicago's Lake Shore Drive, protesting the city's continued inattention to inferior schooling. By 1965, however, Chicago protesters were able to draw on a provision in the 1964 Civil Rights Act that allowed federal authorities to freeze funding until the city addressed their grievances, but they were thwarted once again when Mayor Richard J. Daley met personally with President Johnson who, eager to secure Daley's support for his reelection, approved the release of those funds. This scenario—so similar to how established powers had responded to the Mississippi Challenge the year before—further underscored the limits of legislative victories and conventional party politics.

Thus did activists in Chicago and other northern cities come to a similar disillusionment not only with racial integration as a desirable or workable goal but also with conventional politics as a way to achieve it. At the same time, many lost faith in a social movement strategy premised on Gandhian nonviolence as an effective impetus for social change. Neither integration nor nonviolence had ever been fully embraced by a majority of southern Movement activists nor by the larger, more pragmatic and skeptical black community. There had always been strong doubts as well about integration as the best strategy to achieve better education for black K-12 students (as opposed to college and graduate training). In 1955, for example, a poll of southern blacks had found that just 53 percent approved of the *Brown* ruling mandating integration; many of the skeptics were motivated no doubt by fears of racist harassment of young children and the likelihood that black teachers and administrators would be demoted or fired. By the late 1960s there was ample evidence that both fears were well founded. Consequently, by 1968 protesters' demands had shifted from integration to greater community control of the personnel and curriculum in schools that served the black population. Indicative of the striking shift in demands was a walkout in Chicago that year of an estimated thirty-five thousand students, demanding black history courses, more black teachers and administrators, as well as—surprisingly—"more homework!"

Protests there and in other cities over the next decade reflected not only the rise of new leaders committed to a "black power" agenda, but also the conversion of many of the earlier integrationist activists to similar views. In New York that year, Rev. Milton A. Galamison, head of an NAACP chapter and pastor of the Siloam Presbyterian Church, who had led protests against segregated schooling since the early 1960s, became a convert to community control of the schools in the Ocean Hill-Brownsville section of Brooklyn. With the support of John Lindsay, the newly elected liberal Republican mayor, experimental schools were organized, but they soon encountered determined opposition from the city's teachers' union, which objected to community control over teacher evaluations and placements. Since not only were the majority of long-tenured teachers white, but many were also Jewish, the policy conflict turned into an ugly and bitter racial conflict that set former allies at odds.

Meanwhile in Chicago, Rev. Arthur Brazier, the minister of the Apostolic Church of God and a prominent leader in the 1966 Chicago Freedom Movement, who had long campaigned for integrated schools, had lost faith in that solution and had become an advocate of community control. With funding from the federal poverty program, the Woodlawn Experimental Schools Project (WESP) was established in August 1964 to direct an experiment in community control of that area's public schools. Developed in partnership with the Chicago Public Schools and the University of Chicago, WESP hired a veteran teacher and principal, Barbara Sizemore, to direct the experiment.

Although Sizemore was not opposed to integration in principle, she strongly rejected the inference of black inferiority in plans to bus black children out of their neighborhoods in order to achieve it. On the other hand, as an elementary school teacher since the early 1950s and principal of Anton Dvorak Elementary School since 1963, Sizemore had wrestled with the impact of overcrowding on black children's educational prospects: By 1965, Dvorak was cramming 1,400 pupils into thirty-four classrooms. The Woodlawn project freed her to experiment with administrative policies such as collective decision making in which parents and students as well as teachers and administrators had a voice. Echoing—and likely influenced by the Mississippi

Freedom School project—WESP adopted community-oriented curricula and teaching techniques under Sizemore's leadership.

Although WESP did not encounter the fierce resistance that undercut the Ocean Hills–Brownsville experiment, the project was defunded after only three years, underscoring the fragile financial support for alternative schools, whether public or private. Student movements at all levels of education continued to foster curricular reforms in the city, however, emphasizing black history, arts, and culture. Indeed, 1969 opened onto a decade of agitation in colleges and universities across the nation as students—many of them shaped by experiences in the southern movement—turned their attention to similar curricular and administrative reforms on college and university campuses.

Housing

Broad structural changes in the racial dynamics of urban life also undergirded the growing skepticism about the efficacy or even the desirability of integration of public schools. Most striking were the dramatic changes in urban demography and the spatial relations of inner cities with exurban communities. Ironically, labor and residential patterns in the Jim Crow South had promoted far greater interracial contact than in northern and western cities historically, a feature of southern life that had long surprised and often repelled northern white visitors. Similarly, several turn-of-the-century northern and border cities developed residential patterns wherein blacks resided in extensive settlements in the rear alleys of city blocks while whites occupied their street fronts. As southern black out-migration quickened, however, spatial separation at work and home intensified, evolving by midcentury into rigid political and economic as well as spatial boundaries between white suburbs and black inner cities.

The impact of these changes, first felt in urban public school systems as residential separation within cities and finally between cities and their surrounding suburbs, thwarted integration initiatives. Four years before the *Brown* decision, for example, the population of Chicago's Woodlawn neighborhood had been 86 percent white; by 1960 it was almost 90 percent black. Often the change in residential patterns transpired with disorienting rapidity. For example, Spencer Elementary went from 80 percent white to 80 percent black in just four years.

The sudden changes in school demographics over the postwar decades were a direct consequence of changing urban housing patterns, much of which were underwritten by federal policies and subsidies, as well as "white flight." The "black metropolis" dreams of the 1920s and 1930s were ravaged by postwar urban renewal projects that displaced 160,000 black Chicagoans from their homes between 1945 and 1965, with only a small number (3,100) relocated into public housing. Home ownership in black neighborhoods was made more difficult still by federal and commercial banking policies denying conventional mortgages to prospective buyers and by violent resistance to their making purchases in white neighborhoods. Not only were lending rates higher, but many aspiring black homeowners were forced into loan arrangements that deprived them of the opportunity to build wealth through property ownership. Typically, black purchasers were systematically forced into "purchase contracts" rather than conventional mortgages that would have allowed them to build equity in a property over time. Moreover, well into the postwar era, even those who could secure normal mortgages were terrorized by violent white resistance. In the summer of 1951, for example, four thousand white rioters threatened the life of Harvey Clark, a black veteran who had moved into an apartment in Cicero, an all-white neighborhood in Chicago. Thus did a combination of racist public policies and vigilante violence sustain racial enclaves in the urban North.

Violent conflicts over racial turf were dramatic evidence of northern Jim Crow, but less spectacular, seemingly racially neutral developments were rapidly consolidating a racially divided nation. Increased residential segregation reflected broader systemic changes in American life, including suburban growth and the relocation of industrial and commercial activity and employment outside city limits, all of which were made feasible by federally funded postwar highway construction. The result was a literal hardening of the spatial and institutional divisions between black and white America. As with school integration, these systemic changes complicated and arguably eventually defeated northern protest movements that sought to reverse the trend.

Racial discrimination in northern housing markets, which was a factor shaping access both to integrated schools and to the job market, became another front in the general mobilization for racial equality during the 1950s and 1960s. NAACP lawyers had filed suits challenging housing discrimination during the same period that school segregation cases were working their way through federal courts. Although the 1948 Supreme Court case *Shelly v. Kramer* outlawed restrictive covenants—riders on purchase contracts prohibiting reselling a property to blacks—the federal government's housing programs were administered in ways that lent continued support not only to their own racially discriminatory loan policies but also to those of private lenders. Even the Civil Rights Act of 1964 explicitly exempted discriminatory FHA mortgages from legal scrutiny, and not until the summer of 1968 was federal legislation passed to address housing discrimination explicitly. Like many previous reform measures, however, the Fair Housing Act of 1968 ultimately proved ineffective.

In fact, during the brief interval between the passage of the landmark Civil Rights Act of 1964 and the housing law in 1968, a powerful backlash against further efforts to achieve racial equality emerged in political jurisdictions previously sympathetic to the Movement. In California, for example, a fair housing measure passed in 1963 was effectively rejected by 65 percent of the voters in a referendum the very next year; the same electorate had cast

60 percent of its votes for Lyndon Johnson on the presidential ballot. Notwithstanding repeated disappointments on the legal front, however, the major civil rights organizations continued to mount direct-action campaigns challenging housing discrimination throughout the postwar decades.

Perhaps it was Chicago's long history of direct-action protests that made it an attractive candidate for Martin Luther King Jr.'s SCLC when it decided to bring the tactics of the southern movement north. Rather than targeting public accommodations and voting rights, however, the campaign would continue the Chicago Freedom Movement's ongoing focus on housing discrimination, but with Birmingham-style mass street marches designed to extract concessions from city authorities. In July 1966, after moving into an apartment in Chicago's West Side ghetto, King held a mass rally at Soldier Field and led a protest march to city hall. In subsequent demonstrations, protesters marched through the city's segregated enclaves, where they were violently assaulted by white residents. On July 30, 350 people marching through Gage Park were attacked with bricks and stones. Unlike similar events in the South, these tactics failed to arouse national support for the protesters' demands. Rioting that summer on the city's West Side is likely to have further alienated many of those who previously had been sympathetic (or at least indifferent) to the Chicago Movement's goals. Absent broader public support, negotiations with city authorities proved fruitless. Indeed, Mayor Daley, strengthened by his alliance with the Johnson administration and enjoying the backing of some black elected officials dependent on the city's Democratic machine, was able to offer King's movement concessions that soon proved illusory because there was no means of enforcing them. Outmaneuvered, King ended his campaign. This outcome further alienated other Movement activists from traditional protest tactics. Later that fall, when SNCC and CORE protesters undertook a march through the Cicero neighborhood, they explicitly rejected any commitment to nonviolence.

Even as some Movement activists were mobilizing open-housing campaigns, however, others—in a pattern similar to that of the education activists—turned inward to buttress the internal resources of black communities. Jesse Gray's tenants' rights campaign in New York's Harlem community exemplifies that turn. A World War II veteran of the US Merchant Marine and an organizer for the National Maritime Union after the war, Gray began his activist career as a socialist, but in later years became allied with Malcolm X, who rejected integration and favored a black nationalist approach to racial divisions. In fact, Gray, who was a leader of open-housing demonstrations during the 1950s and had been active in the American Labor Party's efforts to organize tenants' unions, had also soured on integrationist projects by the early 1960s and become increasingly skeptical of alliances with liberal whites. By the mid-1960s, he had turned his attention to independent efforts to achieve housing rights for inner-city tenants, organizing rent strikes to demand enforcement of building codes, regular garbage pickups, and rat abatement programs. He gained national attention when he led a protest that dumped dead rats at a Manhattan courthouse. Aided by a federal poverty program that funded legal services for the poor, Gray's organization filed class-action lawsuits to force the city to improve the housing conditions of ghetto residents. Once again, movement activism in the North shifted the targets and objectives away from integration per se to mobilizing the internal resources of black communities seeking remediation of their conditions.

Jobs

It is often forgotten that the initial proposal for a march on the nation's capital in 1963 was made by the venerable labor and civil rights leader A. Philip Randolph, with the intent of targeting the growing economic malaise in African American communities. The Civil Rights Act passed in response to the march did include provisions to address discrimination in employment. By the early 1960s, however, it was already evident to many social scientists and civil rights activists that ameliorating prejudicial hiring practices was an insufficient remedy for the unemployment then ravaging black communities. The jobs in southern agriculture that had absorbed the labor of the overwhelming majority of African Americans for three centuries were rapidly disappearing as federal crop support policies initiated during the Great Depression stimulated an acceleration of mechanized production, leading ever-growing numbers of displaced workers to migrate to northern and southern cities. The jobs they sought to fill, however, were just as rapidly migrating out of those cities to the suburbs, and in some cases eventually to foreign locales. Once again, a problem of racial injustice arose that traditional Movement tactics proved ill equipped to address.

These developments complicated traditional protest strategies and tactics, leading some activists to seek alternative solutions. For Leon Sullivan, pastor of North Philadelphia's Zion Baptist Church, the solution was retraining workers and promoting black businesses in the inner city to employ them. Rev. Sullivan's career as a social activist had begun in New York City in the 1940s with Randolph's March on Washington Movement. In the early 1960s he was still organizing sympathy protests supporting the Greensboro sit-in and leading boycotts protesting job discrimination by Philadelphia businesses. Despite winning some concessions, by 1964 Sullivan had come to recognize union discrimination and structural barriers such as automation as equally daunting barriers to black employment. To address these issues, he formed the Opportunities Industrialization Center to seek private and public funding to provide job training and compensatory adult education for unemployed blacks. By the late 1960s, Sullivan's program embraced the promotion of black-owned inner-city businesses as an additional strategy to address urban unemployment. Sullivan's trajectory reflected a broader and increasingly popular embrace of black capitalism as a strategy for achieving equal justice. It was a strategy that attracted some funding and ideological support from white Republicans (including most notably President Richard Nixon) and a growing number of black conservatives.

Unlike many black self-help initiatives, however, Sullivan's initiative depended ultimately on federal funding and private philanthropy. Just forty-four days after passing civil rights legislation in 1964, Congress had approved the creation of the Office of Economic Opportunity to wage what Johnson had christened a "war on poverty." Activist-oriented authors of the legislation had managed to include the unprecedented requirement that poor people themselves be represented on the boards that planned and executed community projects, which made these positions targets for and sources of employment for community activists. By the same logic, former civil rights activists were drawn into poverty programs as traditional Movement activism subsided and issues of economic justice took center stage. Many activists also recognized that these community action agencies could provide an institutional basis for conventional political mobilizations as well as more community-based agendas.

These unanticipated features of poverty legislation created persistent tensions with established politicians, who were at best lukewarm to sharing power with their poor black constituents and in many instances fiercely hostile to the prospect. Even such popular programs as legal services for the poor and preschool education in Head Start drew opposition. Legal aid agencies filed class-action suits challenging government policies, and Head Start provided employment that local politicians could not control. Big-city mayors wanted the patronage and supplements to their budgets that poverty funding supported, but not the threats to their power such independent agencies might pose. Thus was the generally agreed need to reverse the ongoing job drain from cities compromised by the perceived threat that effective programs might pose to established powers.

Politics

The passage of the Voting Rights Act in August 1965, which mandated direct intervention by federal officers to register black voters, not only achieved a half-century-long civil rights objective but was also a victory etched in scenes showing black southerners inundating voter registration tables in jurisdictions that had once terrorized them. Former SNCC staffer Julian Bond won a seat representing Atlanta in the Georgia legislature, and over the decade following passage of the Voting Rights Act many other civil rights veterans—among them John Lewis, Marion Barry, and Andrew Young—would be drawn into conventional politics as well. The disheartening defeat of the Lowndes County Freedom Party candidates in 1966 signaled the daunting challenges black political aspirants still faced in the rural Deep South, despite their huge demographic advantages, but four years later John Hulett was elected sheriff of Lowndes County and two other founding members of the Lowndes County Black Panther Party won other offices as well. However, the lag between the earlier defeat and subsequent victory made clear that the South's elected political leadership would not be transformed overnight.

Ironically, it was in northern cities that the political resurgence of black politicians would emerge almost immediately. In 1967, just two years after the law's passage, Richard Hatcher and Carl Stokes won mayoral contests in Gary, Indiana, and Cleveland, Ohio, respectively. Over the next seven years, black candidates won mayoral elections in Newark (1970), Los Angeles (1973), and Detroit (1974). These victories had less to do with the expansion of voting rights per se than mobilizations around civil rights issues across the nation, the rapid changes in the racial demography of major cities, and, perhaps in some cases, the urban rebellions during the late 1960s that had shaken the political status quo in many of these cities. In any case, scores of black officeholders were eventually added to Congress and to state legislatures, including several from southern districts politically transformed by earlier civil rights mobilizations.

The emergence of black officeholders coincided, however, with a rapid decline of most of the insurgent organizations that had led those voter mobilizations over the previous decade. The southern-based organizations, SCLC and SNCC, faltered in their attempts to establish bases in the urban North, while the traditionally northern-based groups, CORE and the NAACP, underwent difficult transitions as they attempted to adapt to the rapidly changing political environment. Urban riots, growing black militancy, and a fierce white backlash fed a conservative shift in national politics that recast the traditional arguments for racial equality. All of the major civil rights organizations confronted declining financial support and leadership crises.

SNCC was bankrupted, in part by the backlash against Stokely Carmichael's militant "black power" slogan, which he had unleashed during the Meredith march in 1966. Black Power reshaped the debate over equal rights for the next decade, but the opposition it aroused among more cautious black as well as white allies undercut SNCC's fundraising and led Carmichael to resign as chair in May 1967. He was succeeded by H. Rap Brown, who became embroiled in controversy for allegedly inciting a riot in Cambridge, Maryland, and was later sent to federal prison for life following a highly suspect conviction for murder in Georgia. In April 1969, after a brief, abortive attempt to form an alliance with the Black Panther Party, Carmichael was ousted from SNCC altogether and sought refuge in Guinea.

At CORE, chairman James Farmer was replaced in 1966 by the more militant Floyd McKissick, who in turn was succeeded after two years by Roy Innis. Innis's incoherent blend of black nationalism and conservatism, as reflected in his simultaneous support of Richard Nixon in 1972 and Uganda's dictator Idi Amin, soon rendered that organization politically irrelevant as well. Of the original "big five" who had led the March on Washington in 1963, therefore, only the relatively conservative National Urban League and NAACP would survive beyond the 1970s, but the latter's membership was less than half its former size and the national influence of both organizations was much reduced.

One could argue that the hollowing out of the traditional civil rights leadership was as much a result of the exodus of key leaders to other domains, including conventional politics and the public sector, as it was a consequence of ideological declension. Several leaders moved into electoral politics or managed the campaigns to elect their fellow activists, often deploying skills learned during earlier insurgencies to mobilize voting constituencies. Others took positions in the public sector, the nonprofit sector, or on university faculties. John Lewis and Julian Bond built political careers on their earlier civil rights fame with constituents who knew them well. Although SNCC's first chairman, Marion Barry, was a newcomer to the nation's capital in 1965, he mobilized a bus boycott against a powerful business monopolist there and, with the help of fellow SNCC veteran Ivanhoe Donaldson, parlayed that victory into a long tenure as the city's mayor. Other big-city mayors, Newark's Kenneth Gibson in the 1970s and Chicago's Harold Washington in the 1980s, owed their mayoral careers to supporters and constituents who had gained skills in community organizing during the Movement. Although the task of governing proved fundamentally different from winning office, there were some continuities nonetheless between civil rights insurgencies and conventional politics.

The Poor People's Campaign

The decline of the traditional civil rights organizations might be explained, paradoxically, as both a mark of their successful assault on the Jim Crow regime that had strangled black life since the end of Reconstruction and a consequence of their inability to adjust to the new struggles black Americans confronted in the aftermath of that victory. If true, then 1968 may well have signaled the critical onset of that denouement. Shortly after the new year, SCLC began planning for another massive march on Washington, but this time focused more fully on issues of economic justice and intent on mobilizing a truly multiracial crusade. Dr. King announced these plans at a press conference on December 4, 1967, aware no doubt of the symbolic significance of that date: It fell on the eve of the twelfth anniversary of his historic speech launching the Montgomery bus boycott at Holt Street Baptist Church.

Not only had the objectives and character of the Civil Rights Movement changed in the interval, however, but 1968 also proved a watershed moment in world history. A rapid succession of events, foreign as well as domestic, shaped the context for King's final effort to demonstrate the efficacy of interracial alliances and nonviolence as tools to remedy social injustice. In that year popular movements for social change ricocheted across the globe, with mobilizations in Mexico City and Paris shaking a postwar world order already reeling from decolonization movements in Asia and Africa. Particularly notable for the classic civil rights struggle, Gandhian precepts of social change appeared to many outdated or irrelevant, seeding a caustic reception to tactics of nonviolent resistance. Nonetheless, defenders of nonviolence could point to the corrosive effects of violence in the ongoing war to underscore the practical as well as the moral logic of their creed.

And, indeed, over a forty-day period in early spring, the world seemed turned upside down. On March 1, news reports announced the imminent publication of the report of the Kerner Commission that had been appointed by President Johnson to study and recommend solutions to the wave of urban rebellions that had swept American cities between 1964 and 1967. The report concluded that "white racism is essentially responsible for the explosive mixture which has been accumulating in our cities since the end of World War II," an analysis it coupled with the stark warning that America was being rapidly transformed into "two societies, one black, one white, separate and unequal," pointedly the stark opposite of what recent civil rights victories and public policy reforms had ostensibly sought to achieve. Moreover, the commission noted that the estimated price tag for further, more thoroughgoing reforms amounted to merely a third of the cost of the ongoing war in Vietnam. But in the competition between guns and butter, as it was often termed, butter invariably lost.

Meanwhile, ongoing events in Vietnam, initiated by a bold North Vietnamese military offensive launched a month earlier, during the Tet New Year, had left American forces shocked and disoriented, effectively confirming for many military analysts that America was losing the war and could expect only a stalemate at best. This event upended conventional political expectations as well when Senator Eugene McCarthy won the support of 42 percent of New Hampshire's Democratic primary voters, thus casting doubt on Lyndon Johnson's grip on his party's nomination and drawing Robert Kennedy into the race on March 16. On March 31, Johnson announced that he would not be a candidate for reelection that fall. Four days later Martin Luther King Jr. was assassinated in Memphis, Tennessee.

Throughout this rapid concatenation of events, therefore, the war in Vietnam continued to frame the political context in which social justice issues were debated, even if its impact on the reception of nonviolent doctrine remains somewhat speculative. At the very moment the Poor People's Campaign was being organized, American soldiers brutally massacred Vietnamese villagers at My Lai. Although that event was not publicly exposed until years later, it reflects the difficulty of promoting a nonviolent campaign against a background of wartime violence playing out nightly on American TV news programs. There were fears that the war's violence was, in one way or another, being brought back home. Indeed, the submerged warfare in America's inner cities to which the Kerner Commission had responded fed those fears.

It is hardly coincidental, therefore, that it was following a massive protest against the Vietnam War at the Pentagon on October 23, 1967, that Martin Luther King Jr. had first floated the possibility of a demonstration in the nation's capital to highlight the country's neglect of entrenched poverty. Modeled on the Bonus Marches staged by unemployed veterans in the early 1920s, thousands of demonstrators would pitch tents on the Washington Mall until the government responded to their demands. Apparently the germ of King's idea had emerged a month earlier during a tension-filled debate at an SCLC strategy conference held at Airlie House in Virginia, when Marian Wright (later Edelman) proposed a greater focus on black impoverishment as an alternative to redoubling efforts in Chicago (favored by Jesse Jackson), increasing southern voter registration (favored by Hosea Williams), or shifting resources to antiwar protests (favored by James Bevel). King found merit in Wright's argument that addressing poverty— "uplifting the invisible poor" in places like Mississippi—should be a Movement priority, and he was fascinated by the prospect of bringing their "faces and stories" to national attention and making the poor politically visible. Apparently Wright's suggestion to take the 1932 Bonus Marchers as a model might also have inspired the campaign to become multiethnic and bi-racial. Thus the march sought to incorporate participants from the emerging American Indian Movement and the ongoing Chicano movement led by Cesar Chavez, as well as highlighting the more general problem of poverty by including rural southern whites, whose impoverished conditions President Johnson had focused on three years earlier as he sought to gain broad support for his antipoverty program.

It may well be that King thought of this as the Movement's last campaign, in both a temporal sense and because of its all-encompassing social justice agenda. The ambitious agenda was reflected in the fact that, in King's words, "poverty was bigger than race." For him it also presented an opportunity to demonstrate the continued relevance and efficacy of nonviolent social protest to address unjust regimes and human suffering. By the late 1960s, however, both nonviolence and cross-racial solidarity had become much less attractive to many social activists, possibly including some in King's own SCLC. It would soon become evident that the proposed march was destined to confront not only a weakened ideological commitment to nonviolence among black activists but also the difficulty organizing poor folk for a campaign outside their familiar communities. Thus, while King was welcomed enthusiastically by poor black folk in small rural communities in the South, he found it difficult to convince many of them to journey to far-off Washington to demonstrate. Indeed, at times these problems so discouraged King that in despair he considered calling off the campaign altogether.

A moment's reflection might have reminded him that previous mobilizations had been grounded in specific communities and supported by local institutions, notwithstanding their material impoverishment. It is clear that the project's lack of community grounding also complicated fundraising and the maintenance of nonviolent discipline. Notwithstanding the crucial contributions that earlier campaigns had received from outside funding sources, the local communities themselves were the first and last resort, especially since some of those resources were in-kind contributions of meals and beds that people of modest means were often able to supply. And although sustaining nonviolent discipline had been a problem from the very beginning, as episodes in Montgomery and Birmingham demonstrated, those cities also showed that order could often be restored by appeals to local knowledge and bonds of trust. But such resources and strategies would be less available in a far-flung national mobilization. Indeed, some of the very problems feared in the original planning of the march in 1963 would be magnified during the lengthy encampment on the Mall during the summer of 1968.

Although the campaign's focus on the poor was clearly aimed at addressing the fundamental economic policy issues that had taken center stage in social movements by the late 1960s, it was less clear how the march's specific demands for government action would be framed. As Bevel was fond of saying, "There was nothing unconstitutional about starving." For decades Randolph had been agitating for a government response to employment discrimination and unemployment, and more recently the Urban League's new director, Whitney Young, had urged the equivalent of the postwar Marshall Plan to ensure that black Americans did not end up, as he put it, with "a mouthful of rights and an empty stomach." More recently the idea of substituting a guaranteed income for welfare checks had gained traction with some white sociologists as well as black radicals. But the broad tent of participants was likely to ultimately lead to differences over priorities.

King's almost inadvertent entanglement in a local labor dispute in Memphis, Tennessee, postponed the necessity to address many of these impending tensions, albeit with ultimately tragic results. Nashville Movement veteran James Lawson urged King to lend his support to an ongoing strike of black sanitation workers in Memphis, where since 1961 he had been pastor of the Centenary United Methodist Church. The prospect of King getting involved in the strike was hotly opposed by some of the SCLC staff, who feared it would be a distraction and further delay the already delayed campaign. King correctly viewed Memphis as "the Washington campaign in miniature," however. And, indeed, the "garbage workers' strike" graphically captured the main themes of the Poor People's Campaign as expressed in the lived experience of ordinary workers. Their victimization by impoverishment and disrespect merged issues of racial injustice and poverty, which they captured succinctly in their slogan, "I Am A Man!" Memphis was also a convenient and symbolic starting point for an already planned tour of the Mississippi Delta designed to publicize the Poor People's March.

On the other hand, King did indeed become ensnarled in the Memphis strike, especially after one of the marches he led turned violent, raising inconvenient anxieties about the much larger and longer demonstration planned for Washington. Memphis thus became the opening skirmish of the larger campaign, and he could not abandon it. As the nation was still trying to come to terms with President Johnson's shocking announcement on March 31 that he would not run for reelection, King returned to Memphis intent on leading a "redemptive" march to prove once again that nonviolent action could address the nation's ills.

On April 4, four days before the rescheduled demonstration intended to redeem nonviolent protest, King was assassinated. Black communities in more than a hundred cities went up in flames that evening, including in the nation's capital, where machine guns were mounted around the Capitol building. The following Tuesday, King's body was interred in Atlanta, after

11. During the Poor People's Campaign, the mule-drawn wagon became the emblem of the endemic poverty, especially in the rural South, to which the Movement sought to bring national attention. Just three months earlier, a wagon like this one had served as the caisson carrying Martin Luther King Jr. to his grave.

public services at his alma mater, Morehouse College. King's funeral procession marched behind a mule-driven wagon carrying his body, a lasting symbol of the new movement he had sought to begin.

Wagons like it would bring some of the three thousand poor people who came to Washington the following month. The demonstrators pitched tents on the Mall, which they named "Resurrection City." Although they engaged in some lobbying of Congress and government agencies, they did not engage in the acts of civil disobedience that King had originally envisioned. (Some activists had originally thought of using such tactics in the 1963 March on Washington as well, but they were dissuaded.) The encampment encountered logistical problems, police surveillance, and disruptions from suspected provocateurs from the FBI's Counter Intelligence Program (COINTELPRO), whose infiltration of protest demonstrations had by then become standard practice. Demoralized and depleted after a six-week occupation of the Mall, and with the expiration of their license to camp there, the protesters were forcefully removed by police and National Guardsmen. Their petition for economic justice was ignored.

Chapter 6
Legacies: "Freedom is a constant struggle"

Although most historians would agree with Jacqueline Dowd Hall's characterization of the Civil Rights Movement as "the most remarkable mass movement in American history," popular retrospectives tend to be more mixed, very often obscuring the very qualities that Hall hoped might enable it to speak to current challenges. Seeking to mute that voice, erstwhile staunch defenders of the racial status quo have taken to quoting selective passages from Martin Luther King Jr.'s speeches to sustain their reactionary views. Meanwhile generations of black youth born in the Movement's aftermath are apt to be critical of its accomplishments, given the continued salience of a racial order that demeans their worth and limits their life prospects. And the powerful influence that the Movement exerted on other social movements during the second half of the twentieth century, as well as on American thought and culture more generally, is often underestimated, if not ignored altogether.

But the history recounted here demonstrates that the Movement experience itself shaped the values, perspectives, and vision of its participants as much as—and likely more than—the titular leaders who sought to determine its objectives and shape its course. Arguably, its enduring impact on the lives and consciousness of ordinary people is the message conveyed by a Movement song that became popular by the mid-1960s, as the martyrs to its cause mounted. "Freedom," it declares, "is a constant struggle.... O Lord I've struggled so long that I must be free." In a book that draws its title from this song, Angela Davis argues that depicting the Movement as merely the work of heroic individuals risks leading future generations to misrecognize their own capacity to act collectively to achieve social justice, an observation that underscores the principal theme of this book.

Although it is true that the Movement did not—could not—completely overturn the racial bias and inequality that had been lodged in America's democratic experiment since the nation's founding, it did succeed in destroying the apartheid-like forms of the social order that had emerged at the dawn of the twentieth century. That social order posed a lethal obstacle to any black southerner who even attempted to challenge an impoverished and devalued life. At the very least, then, the Movement, as the song quoted in the previous paragraph suggests, prepared the ground for future generations' struggles to make a more just society, to make black lives matter.

The case for the influence of the Movement on other social movements is more complex, but it, too, must be assessed in historical perspective. The twentieth-century course of social movements whose trajectories stretched back to earlier decades and even back to the nineteenth century were influenced or reinvigorated by the civil rights struggles of the 1960s. The American campaigns for women's rights, for example, were an outgrowth of women's active roles in the radical antislavery movement that began two decades before the Civil War. It was through those experiences that a remarkable cohort of white and black women leaders asserted their right even to speak in public and subsequently laid claim to the right to vote. Sometimes allied, sometimes hostile, the mutual aspirations of black and white feminists over the century following the Civil War formed a historical preamble for the women's movements that emerged after World War II. But that new generation of feminists pursued a different, more militant agenda in the latter half of the twentieth century. No doubt their reorientation owed much to the dynamics of their own lived experiences in postwar America, but since much of its leadership at that point had come of age during the Movement years, and in fact many had been witnesses to or active in that Movement, it is likely that they found resonances there in what was transpiring around them. As the experiences of Ella Baker and other activists show, the Movement itself was not free of gender biases, but this, too, could and did become an inspiration for feminist activism. Certainly some of the black women activists coming of age during the Civil Rights Movement drew on those experiences to give shape to a black feminist agenda.

Probably the most immediate and direct influence of the Movement was on the student rebellions during the 1960s on

12. As its leadership shifted to a more militant generation, the women's liberation movement adopted some of the tactics of the Civil Rights Movement, as in this march down New York City's Fifth Avenue on August 27, 1970 (one day before the seventh anniversary of the March on Washington).

college campuses across the nation, black as well as white. In these cases, the links to Movement activists is often clear and direct. The first of these student movements emerged at the University of California at Berkeley in September 1964, just a month after the Mississippi Challenge at the Democratic national convention. Mario Savio had only recently returned from the Freedom Summer project when he rose on December 2, 1964, to urge Berkeley students gathered on Sproul Plaza to take direct action to force the university to address their grievances concerning the very character and purpose of their education. In his audience were several others who had endured the same harrowing experiences in Mississippi that summer as he had. Just months later a parallel student movement emerged at Howard University, the unwitting incubator of field workers for SNCC and CORE earlier in that decade. On both black and white campuses, student demands would evolve over time from campus-specific issues to broader challenges to school curricula, governance, and what many students saw as their school's tacit support of the Vietnam War. Among their specific demands were curricular changes to recognize the historical and contemporary place of black people in American society.

Native American struggles for justice stretched back to the earliest days of the American republic, but even then the respective struggles of black and red Americans for freedom and respect were often interlinked, albeit sometimes as friends, sometimes as foes. But the modern American Indian Movement was founded in July 1968, just months after Dr. King had welcomed Native Americans into the coalition formed to launch the Poor People's Campaign. Just a year later, when a new pan-Indian group, the Indians of All Tribes, launched a nineteen-month occupation of the recently abandoned Alcatraz Island in the San Francisco Bay, their occupation drew support from black as well as white equal rights activists in the Bay Area, especially from the student movement at San Francisco State University. The 1970s opened onto a series of similar protests by Native American groups, including a seventy-one-day occupation of Pine Ridge Reservation, the site of the infamous Wounded Knee massacre of Indians by American army units in 1890. The "Longest Walk," a march from California to Washington in 1978 to protest a congressional proposal to extinguish Indian treaty rights, was likewise a striking echo of the Poor People's March exactly a decade earlier.

Other initiatives during what some have dubbed the "red power" era of Native American protests resemble the shifting perspectives and objectives of diverse African American social movements during the late 1960s and early 1970s. In 1979, the American Indian Movement established an Opportunities Industrialization Center to train Native American workers for the new economy, while other groups established "survival schools" to teach and revitalize traditional Indian cultures and advocate for greater control of the institutions in their communities, all initiatives that Leon Sullivan and Jesse Gray would have recognized and commended.

The Chicano Movement that arose in the 1960s likewise had roots in the mid-nineteenth and early twentieth centuries, but grew more militant in the wake of Cesar Chavez's United Farmworkers Union campaign. Founded in 1962, Chavez's union embraced a philosophy and tactics very similar to the Gandhian approaches advocated by Martin Luther King Jr.'s SCLC. By the late 1960s, however, more militant groups emerged, who much like black groups of that era were not philosophically committed to nonviolence. Representatives of the militant Chicano groups were incorporated uneasily into the Poor People's Campaign, for example. Such tensions were part of a long history of relations between blacks and Mexican Americans. Even as they fought similar battles against segregated schools and other public accommodations during the 1940s and 1950s, for example, African Americans and Mexican Americans often ended up on opposite sides of the legal argument, especially in contexts where

Mexican Americans sought to take advantage of their putative legal status as "white" to gain access to privileges otherwise denied to black Americans.

Although that particular source of intergroup tensions became much less salient with changes in their relative political statuses by midcentury, a common political front could never be taken for granted. Nonetheless, the final decades of the twentieth century witnessed numerous examples of fruitful alliances between black and diverse Latinx communities. Careful opinion surveys and actual voting patterns have consistently shown that their historical differences had become much less politically important, making coalition politics—formal and tacit—more viable. The most striking evidence of this phenomenon is found in the political coalitions forged by Harold Washington's mayoral campaign in Chicago in 1983 and Barack Obama's presidential campaign in 2008.

In sum, the post-Movement dynamics of the struggle to change the nation's racialized social order have been no less fraught and complicated than what preceded it. It was but a different phase of a continuing struggle—a struggle whose core assertion across many decades was that black lives mattered, a repeated challenge to state actions and individual abuses that have long demeaned and disrespected a claim to basic human rights. It is a claim that sparked moments of individual and collective rebellions at various moments over the past two centuries, a claim that each generation seems called on to repeat. Thus does it echo the protean insight of the civil rights song, "Freedom is a constant struggle." It was no accident that the seemingly plaintive refrain of that song became increasingly popular as the struggles of the 1960s grew more intractable and the list of Movement martyrs grew longer. On picket lines and in mass meetings ordinary folk voiced a hard lesson handed down from generations past. Freedom is a prize won not in a single campaign, but in a long struggle waged by a determined and committed people. And, ultimately, it is not exceptional leaders but ordinary people themselves, conscious of the historical possibilities of their moment and acting collectively, who have the capacity to win that fight and change their world. Thus framed as a summons to continued struggle, the song's plaintive cadence is subtly transformed, giving way to an undaunted resolve, resonant with the tempo of a people marching.

References

Introduction

This story was told to author by Catherine Fitzgerald Holt, my mother and Carrie's youngest daughter.

Rebecca J. Scott has documented that the links between claims to citizenship rights and freedom from insult in public accommodations have a deep history in African American thought. See "Discerning a Dignitary Offense: The Concept of Equal 'Public Rights' during Reconstruction," *Law and History Review* 38, no. 3 (August 2020): 519–53.

Raymond Arsenault, *Freedom Riders: 1961 and the Struggle for Racial Justice* (Oxford: Oxford University Press, 2006), 11–22.

Shortly after Carrie's fifth birthday democracy would die again, closer to home, in a riot in 1883 aimed at dismantling Danville's short-lived biracial government. For details, see Jane E. Dailey, *Before Jim Crow: The Politics of Race in Postemancipation Virginia* (Chapel Hill: University of North Carolina Press, 2000), 106–31.

The argument to expand the temporal boundaries of the Civil Rights Movement to encompass initiatives for equal rights that occurred before the decade of activism that began with the Montgomery bus boycott was first articulated in Jacquelyn Dowd Hall's thoughtful and immensely influential article, "The Long Civil Rights Movement and the Political Uses of the Past," *Journal of American History* 91 (March 2005): 1233–63. However well intentioned, the notion that the origins of the Movement should embrace events occurring years if not decades earlier has been stretched to such lengths that it undercuts not only its significance as a truly historic rupture but also our capacity to explain what was historically unique about a decade of struggle that even Hall herself describes as "the most remarkable mass movement in American history."

Chapter 1

Patricia Sullivan, *Lift Every Voice: The NAACP and the Making of the Civil Rights Movement* (New York: New Press, 2009), 69, 77, 311, 375, 396, 363, 400, 414, 104, 162, 249–50, 160, 211, 410, 404–405, 264.

For a more detailed discussion of the Jennings case as well as its larger legal and economic context, see Darryl M. Heller, "The Poor Man's Carriage: Street Railways and Their Publics in Brooklyn and New York, 1850–1896" (PhD thesis, University of Chicago, 2012), 81–100.

For more on northern protests, see Philip Foner, "The Battle to End Discrimination against Negroes on Philadelphia Streetcars: Part 1," *Pennsylvania History* 40 (July 1973): 260–90; and James M. McPherson, *The Negro's Civil War* (New York: Vintage, 1965), 255–64.

James M. McPherson, *The Struggle for Equality: Abolitionists and the Negro in the Civil War and Reconstruction* (Princeton: Princeton University Press, 2014).

On the Louisville, Kentucky protests, see Maria Fleming, *A Place at the Table: The Struggle for Equality in America* (New York: Oxford University Press in association with the Southern Poverty Law Center, 2001).

August Meier and Elliott Rudwick, "The Boycott Movement Against Jim Crow Streetcars in the South, 1900–1906," in *Along the Color Line: Explorations in the Black Experience* (Urbana: University of Illinois Press, 1976), 267–89.

On Civil Rights Cases, see Thomas C. Holt, *Children of Fire: A History of African Americans* (New York: Hill & Wang, 2010), 243–45.

On Walden and the Atlanta movement, see Tomiko Brown-Nagin, *Courage to Dissent: Atlanta and the Long History of the Civil Rights Movement* (New York: Oxford University Press, 2011), 83–113.

On Houston and Howard University, see Genna Rae McNeil, *Groundwork: Charles Hamilton Houston and the Struggle for Civil*

Rights (Philadelphia: University of Pennsylvania Press, 1983),
24–34, 49–53, 70–75, 148–50, 113–15, 84–85.

On NAACP in 1940s, see Patricia Sullivan, *Days of Hope: Race and
Democracy in the New Deal Era* (Chapel Hill: University of North
Carolina Press, 1996), 149–51, 212, 175–89, 224–25, 258.

August Meier and Elliott Rudwick, "The First Freedom Ride,"
Phylon, 30, no. 3 (Fall 1969): 219.

For more on Ella Baker, see Barbara Ransby, *Ella Baker and the Black
Freedom Movement: A Radical Democratic Vision* (Chapel Hill:
University of North Carolina Press, 2003).

Meier and Rudwick, "The First Freedom Ride," 213–22; Raymond
Arsenault, *Freedom Riders: 1961 and the Struggle for Racial Justice*
(Oxford: Oxford University Press, 2007), 22–55.

Chapter 2

The ambiguities and contradictions of elite southerners' reactions in
North Carolina—the prototype of the twentieth-century "New
South" mentality—are discussed by William H. Chafe in *Civilities
and Civil Rights: Greensboro, North Carolina, and the Black
Struggle for Freedom* (New York: Oxford University Press,
1980), 56–97.

Throughout his book Myrdal suggests that although racism was a
national problem, it was less entrenched in the North, thus
implying change would be easier and might well begin there.
Gunnar Myrdal, *An American Dilemma: The Negro Problem and
Modern Democracy* (New York: Harper & Brothers, 1944), 1:xlviii,
45–49, 512; 2:603–604, 1010–11, 1014. See also Walter Jackson,
*Gunnar Myrdal and America's Conscience: Social Engineering and
Racial Liberalism, 1938–1987* (Chapel Hill: University of North
Carolina Press, 1990).

Traci Parker, *Department Stores and the Black Freedom Movement:
Workers, Consumers, and Civil Rights from the 1930s to 1980s*
(Chapel Hill: University of North Carolina Press, 2019).

Robert R. Korstad, *Civil Rights Unionism: Tobacco Workers and the
Struggle for Democracy in the Mid-Twentieth-Century South*
(Chapel Hill: University of North Carolina Press, 2003).

These statistics on population changes are based on an analysis of US
census data collected by Alexander Hofmann. It should be noted
that Cambridge was something of an outlier among this group,
since its demographic and economic characteristics were closer to

Deep South towns than the others in this list. For data sources, see *Sixteenth Census of the United States: 1940, Volume. II, Characteristics of the Population (1943)*, Parts 1, 2, 5, 6; *A Report of the Seventeenth Decennial Census of the United States. Census of Population: 1950, Volume II, Characteristics of the Population (1953)*, Parts 2, 4, 10, 11, 1833, 42, 46; *The Eighteenth Decennial Census of the United States, Census of Population: 1960, Volume I, Characteristics of the Population (1963)*, Parts 2, 5, 11, 12, 20, 35, 44, 48.

For more on southern plantation labor controls, see Nan Elizabeth Woodruff, *American Congo: The African American Freedom Struggle in the Delta* (Cambridge, MA: Harvard University Press, 2003).

My statistical analysis is not intended to suggest that the correlations constituted causation but simply that these social changes made sustained resistance possible. For examples of the demands on a plantation employee's nonworking hours, see Thomas C. Holt, *Children of Fire: A History of African Americans* (New York: Hill & Wang, 2010), 250–51.

Kathleen Frydl, *The G.I. Bill* (Cambridge, UK: Cambridge University Press, 2009), 222–62.

For more on the impact of military bases, see J. Mills Thornton, *Dividing Lines: Municipal Politics and the Struggle for Civil Rights in Montgomery, Birmingham, and Selma* (Tuscaloosa: University of Alabama Press, 2002), 412, 420, 465. The story of a black soldier, Buford Holt, who joined the protests in Danville, Virginia, inspired a ballad by SNCC field worker Matthew Jones, entitled "The Demonstrating G.I."

Holt, *Children of Fire*, 296–98, 298; Laurie B. Green, *Battling the Plantation Mentality: Memphis and the Black Freedom Struggle* (Chapel Hill: University of North Carolina Press, 2007), 81–111.

For more on the political situation in Alabama cities, see Thornton, *Dividing Lines*, 20–140, 40, 69–70, 73, 598 n72.

Adam Green, *Selling the Race: Culture, Community, and Black Chicago, 1940–1955* (Chicago: University of Chicago Press, 2007).

In an interview for the video *Eyes on the Prize*, Parks stated that she was thinking of Emmett Till when she refused to give up her seat. T. R. M. Howard had spoken about the murder to an overflow crowd at Dexter Avenue Baptist Church on November 27, a meeting sponsored by Omega Psi Phi fraternity. He was on a speaking tour that included Baltimore, New York City, Los Angeles, Pittsburgh, and Washington, DC. Holt, *Children of Fire*,

293. See also Davis Houck and Matthew Grindy, *Emmett Till and the Mississippi Press* (Jackson: University Press of Mississippi, 2008), x.

Robin D. G. Kelley, "'We Are Not What We Seem': Rethinking Black Working-Class Opposition in the Jim Crow South," *Journal of American History 80*, no. 1 (January 1993); 104.

Taylor Branch, *Parting the Waters: America in the King Years, 1954–63* (New York: Simon & Schuster, 2006), 136–42, 145–46, 151, 158–59, 188, 196, 275, 274–75, 278–80, 295, 276.

On Baton Rouge and Montgomery, see Aldon D. Morris, *The Origins of the Civil Rights Movement: Black Communities Organizing for Change* (New York: Free Press, 1984), 54–63.

Morris, *Origins of the Civil Rights Movement*, 63–68; Branch, *Parting the Waters*, 198.

For more on Greensboro, see William Chafe, *Civilities and Civil Rights: Greensboro, North Carolina, and Black Struggle for Freedom* (New York: Oxford University Press, 1980), 99, 109–41.

Barbara Ransby, *Ella Baker and the Black Freedom Movement: A Radical Democratic Vision* (Chapel Hill: University of North Carolina Press, 2003); Branch, *Parting the Waters*, 291–292.

Charles M. Payne, *I've Got the Light of Freedom: The Organizing Tradition and the Mississippi Freedom Struggle* (Berkeley: University of California Press, 1995).

John Dittmer, *Local People: The Struggle for Civil Rights in Mississippi* (Urbana: University of Illinois Press, 1995), 173. For national figures on demonstrations after Birmingham, see Branch, *Parting the Waters*, 825.

Josephine Baker, freshly arrived from Paris to attend the March on Washington, was among the celebrities introduced to the crowd that day, and several prominent women leaders were also acknowledged—Daisy Bates, Diane Nash Bevel, Rosa Parks, Gloria Richardson, and the widow of Herbert Lee—in a "Tribute to Women." None of these women spoke, however, except for Daisy Bates. Bates acknowledged the group, substituting for Myrlie Evers, Medgar's widow, who had missed her flight. See the program on the National Archives website and Branch, *Parting the Waters*, 880–81.

For more on communities' commitments to violence versus nonviolence, see Charles E. Cobb Jr., *This Nonviolent Stuff'll Get You Killed: How Guns Made the Civil Rights Movement Possible* (Durham, NC: Duke University Press, 2016).

In 1964 an armed group was organized in Louisiana to defend civil rights workers. Lance Hill, *The Deacons for Defense: Armed Resistance and the Civil Rights Movement* (Chapel Hill: University of North Carolina Press, 2004).

Chapter 4

Nan Elizabeth Woodruff, *American Congo: The African American Freedom Struggle in the Delta* (Cambridge, MA: Harvard University Press, 2003), 8–37.

Charles M. Payne, *I've Got the Light of Freedom: The Organizing Tradition and the Mississippi Freedom Struggle* (Berkeley: University of California Press, 1995), 47–50, 155, 270, 227–28, 123–24, 108–11, 118–28, 111, 207–10. See also David T. Beito and Linda Royster Beito, *Black Maverick: T.R.M. Howard's Fight for Civil Rights and Economic Power* (Urbana: University of Illinois Press, 2009), 72–80.

For more on Vera Pigee, see Françoise N. Hamlin, *Crossroads at Clarksdale: The Black Freedom Struggle in the Mississippi Delta after World War II* (Chapel Hill: University of North Carolina Press, 2012), 59–72.

On the murders of Steptoe and Smith and the economic pressures on farm owners like Steptoe, see John Dittmer, *Local People: The*

Struggle for Civil Rights in Mississippi (Urbana: University of
Illinois Press, 1995), 53–54, 106, 109, 187–88.

For detailed discussion of the Mississippi Movement, see Dittmer,
Local People, 170–73, 181–82, 189–90, 106, 109–10, 203, 208–10,
246–47, 251, 250, 251, 258–60, 285–302

Income data found in Dittmer, *Local People*, 125.

Laura Visser-Maessen, *Robert Parris Moses: A Life in Civil Rights and
Leadership at the Grassroots* (Chapel Hill: University of North
Carolina Press, 2016), 54–60, 71–74, 76–89, 168–75.

Such defensive measures had a long history in the South, among the
most dramatic of which was the response to the Atlanta riots in
1906. See Thomas C. Holt, *Children of Fire: A History of African
Americans* (New York: Hill & Wang, 2010), 238–40. On
Mississippi events, see Charles E. Cobb Jr., *This Nonviolent Stuff'll
Get You Killed: How Guns Made the Civil Rights Movement
Possible* (Durham, NC: Duke University Press, 2016).

Clayborne Carson, *In Struggle: SNCC and the Black Awakening of the
1960s* (Cambridge, MA: Harvard University Press, 1995), 41–42.

The COFO project would eventually draw support from a broader
network: lawyers from the National Lawyers Guild for legal help
that the NAACP was sometimes reticent to provide, the Delta
Ministry formed by the National Council of Churches, and the
Medical Committee for Civil Rights to address the endemic health
issues soon to be exposed by Movement volunteers.

Hamlin, *Crossroads at Clarksdale*, 5–6, 65–68, 73, 87.

Western College for Women, which would later merge with Miami
University, was a legatee of the New England migration of
antislavery folk to the Midwest in the antebellum era, which may
partially explain its boldness in hosting an event other area
colleges had shunned.

Jon N. Hale, *The Freedom Schools: Student Activists in the Mississippi
Civil Rights Movement* (New York: Columbia University Press,
2016), 108–48, 196–223.

Taylor Branch, *A Pillar of Fire: America in the King Years, 1963–65*
(New York: Simon & Schuster, 2006), 456–89.

Stokely Carmichael quote from his *Ready for Revolution: The Life and
Struggles of Stokely Carmichael (Kwame Ture)*, with Ekwueme
Michael Thelwell (New York: Simon & Schuster, 2003), chapter 8.

John Lewis quote from his *Walking with the Wind: A Memoir of the
Movement* (New York: Simon & Schuster, 1998), 282–83; Branch,

A *Pillar of Fire*, 474. See also Visser-Maessen, *Robert Parris Moses*, 244–52.

Holt, *Children of Fire*, 324–25.

A march through Mississippi in June 1966 in response to the shooting of James Meredith, for example, was not grounded in any particular community mobilization, nor did it address any specific agent, demanding a concrete legislative or policy objective.

Peniel E. Joseph, *Stokely: A Life* (New York: Basic Civitas, 2014), 81–86.

Hasan Kwame Jeffries, *Bloody Lowndes: Civil Rights and Black Power in Alabama's Black Belt* (New York: New York University Press, 2009), 59, 81–84, 29, 39–41, 46, 79, 167–68.

Taylor Branch, *At Canaan's Edge: America in the King Years, 1965-68* (New York: Simon & Schuster, 2006), 459–60, 494.

Chapter 5

Thomas J. Sugrue, *Sweet Land of Liberty: The Forgotten Struggle for Civil Rights in the North* (New York: Random House, 2008), 290–95, 298–312.

Some individuals, like SNCC's Ivanhoe Donaldson, became involved in the Movement initially while personally delivering food and clothing to oppressed communities in Mississippi. Other prominent activists of northern origin—Bob Moses, Stokely Carmichael, and James Forman—would be drawn to the South by similar commitments.

Evelyn Brooks Higginbotham, foreword to *Freedom North: Black Freedom Struggles outside the South, 1940-1980*, ed. Jeanne F. Theoharis and Komozi Woodard (New York: Palgrave, 2003), x. See also Matthew J. Countryman, *Up South: Civil Rights and Black Power in Philadelphia* (Philadelphia: University of Pennsylvania Press, 2006), 98–119. There were twenty-nine consumer boycotts in Philadelphia alone between 1959 and 1963, a vivid indicator of other frictions wrought by northern urban economies.

Although the most egregious educational inequities were still found in the South, where the systematic provision of public elementary schools for black children outside major cities dated mostly from the 1890s; moreover, in many of those cities public secondary schooling for black adolescents did not exist before the mid- to late 1940s. Indeed, black self-help had accounted for much of the schooling black children did receive before the third decade of the twentieth century, especially in the rural South. During the 1890s and 1910s, desperately impoverished southern black communities had raised more than $3.5 million to match the funding that northern private philanthropists donated to build almost four thousand rural schools. See James D. Anderson, *The Education of Blacks in the South, 1860–1935* (Chapel Hill: University of North Carolina Press, 1988).

For more on Chicago school reform, see Elizabeth Todd-Breland, *A Political Education: Black Politics and Education Reform in Chicago since the 1960s* (Chapel Hill: University of North Carolina Press, 2018), 27–30, 31, 24, 57, 50–55, 77, 61.

For more on African American skepticism about integration, see Tomiko Brown-Nagin, *Courage to Dissent: Atlanta and the Long History of the Civil Rights Movement* (New York: Oxford, 2011), 83–113.

For more background on northern movements, see Sugrue, *Sweet Land of Liberty*, 475–80.

Martha Biondi, *The Black Revolution on Campus* (Berkeley: University of California Press, 2012).

Mark Schultz, *The Rural Face of White Supremacy* (Urbana: University of Illinois Press, 2005), 80–109.

James Borchert, *Alley Life in Washington: Family, Community, Religion, and Folklife in the City, 1850–1970* (Urbana: University of Illinois Press, 1980).

By 1980 black students in Chicago made up 60 percent of the public school population. Todd-Breland, *Political Education*, 41, 151.

For more detailed discussion of federal policies that promoted discrimination, see David M. P. Freund, *Colored Property: State Policy and White Racial Politics in Suburban America* (Chicago: University of Chicago Press, 2007), 99–134, 158–63, 179–97.

Jon Rice, "The World of the Illinois Panthers," in *Freedom North: Black Freedom Struggles Outside the South, 1940–1980*, eds. Jeanne F. Theoharis and Komozi Woodard (New York: Palgrave, 2003), 42. Also see Joshua Bloom and Waldo E. Martin Jr., *Black against Empire: The History and Politics of the Black Panther Party* (Berkeley: University of California Press, 2016).

Rice, "World of the Illinois Panthers," 42; Dalton Conley, *Being Black, Living in the Red: Race, Wealth, and Social Policy in America* (Berkeley: University of California Press, 1999), 55–82.

Thomas C. Holt, *Children of Fire: A History of African Americans* (New York: Hill & Wang, 2010), 349, 345–46, 348–52, 346–47.

See Keeanga-Yamahtta Taylor, *Race for Profit: How Banks and the Real Estate Industry Undermined Black Homeownership* (Chapel Hill: University of North Carolina Press, 2009), 14. I am grateful to Deskin Jenkins for bringing this source to my attention.

Robert O. Self, *American Babylon: Race and the Struggle for Postwar Oakland* (Princeton: Princeton University Press, 2003), 167–68.

Some of CORE's earliest protests had been in opposition to housing bias in newly built settlements in New York's outer boroughs and in other northern cities. It is notable that as CORE-led Freedom Riders made their way to Birmingham in May 1961, twenty-five thousand black residents of Woodlawn boarded forty-six buses for what they also called a "freedom ride" to Chicago's city hall to demand jobs and better housing. Thomas F. Jackson, *From Civil Rights to Human Rights: Martin Luther King, Jr., and the Struggle for Economic Justice, Politics, and Culture in Modern America* (Philadelphia: University of Pennsylvania Press), 136–37; see also August Meier and Elliott Rudwick, *CORE: A Study in the Civil Rights Movement, 1942–1968* (New York: Oxford, 1973).

Taylor Branch, *At Canaan's Edge: America in the King Years, 1965–68* (New York: Simon & Schuster, 2006), 501–22, 655–56, 706, 713–15, 640–43, 720–22, 730, 742; see also James R. Ralph Jr., *Northern Protest: Martin Luther King, Jr., Chicago, and the Civil Rights Movement* (Cambridge, MA: Harvard University Press, 1993), 92–171.

Apparently Randolph's proposed march was only revised to encompass broader issues of racial discrimination at Martin Luther King's initiative in an effort to gain the support of more conservative civil rights leaders such as Roy Wilkins for an omnibus civil rights law. Taylor Branch, *Parting the Waters: America in the King Years, 1954–63* (New York: Simon & Schuster, 2006), 820.

Early examples of the growing trend of jobs moving to the suburbs appeared in Philadelphia shortly after the war, as jobs were moved to suburbs where blacks were denied housing. Holt, *Children of Fire*, 348–50. See also Countryman, *Up South*, 50–57, and Guian McKee, *The Problem of Jobs: Liberalism, Race, and Deindustrialization in Philadelphia* (Chicago: University of Chicago Press, 2008).

For discussion of changes in southern agriculture, see Pete Daniel, *Breaking the Land: The Transformation of Cotton, Tobacco, and*

Rice Cultures since 1880 (Urbana: University of Illinois Press, 1985).

Countryman, *Up South*, 112–19.

President Johnson's phone conversations with Chicago's Mayor Daley and Georgia senator Richard Russell reveals that he shared their opposition to the Office of Economic Opportunity's community action program. Audio records of these calls are held at the Miller Center, University of Virginia, Charlottesville. Consult Presidential Recordings Digital Edition. Johnson Administration, Series: War on Poverty, vol. 2, Miller Center, University of Virginia.

Peniel E. Joseph, *Stokely: A Life* (New York: Basic Civitas, 2014).

For an examples of earlier mobilizations, see Timuel D. Black Jr., *Sacred Ground: The Chicago Streets of Timuel Black as Told to Susan Klonsky*, ed. Bart Schultz (Chicago: Northwestern University Press, 2019).

Report of the National Advisory Commission on Civil Disorders (New York: Bantam Books, 1968).

Daniel S. Lucks, *Selma to Saigon: The Civil Rights Movement and the Vietnam War* (Lexington: University Press of Kentucky, 2014), 73–110.

Quincy Mills, "Raising Hell and Bail: The Danville, Virginia Demonstrations of 1963," unpublished paper presented at University of Chicago Symposium in Honor of Thomas C. Holt, April 2016.

The difficulties SCLC staff faced recruiting marchers, given the project's ambiguous targets and the ever-present fear of sustaining nonviolent discipline, is discussed in Branch, *At Canaan's Edge*, chapter 38.

The firebrand Chicano leader Reies López Tijerina demanded compensation for lands confiscated during the Mexican War. Branch, *At Canaan's Edge*, 717. For more on the broader Chicano farmworkers' movement, see David Montejano, *Quixote's Soldiers: A Local History of the Chicano Movement* (Austin: University of Texas Press, 2010) and Marc S. Rodriguez, *Rethinking the Chicano Movement* (New York: Routledge, 2015).

This FBI counterintelligence project was established in 1956 to conduct surveillance of radical groups. By the late 1960s, however, the agency routinely planted provocateurs to encourage actions that would discredit those groups.

Chapter 6

Jacqueline Dowd Hall, "The Long Civil Rights Movement and the Political Uses of the Past," *Journal of American History 91* (March 2005): 1234.

Angela Y. Davis, *Freedom Is a Constant Struggle: Ferguson, Palestine, and the Foundations of a Movement* (Chicago: Haymarket Books, 2016).

Jean Fagin Yellin and John C. Van Horne, eds., *The Abolitionist Sisterhood: Women's Political Culture in Antebellum America* (Ithaca, NY: Cornell University Press, 1994).

The statement of principles announced by the Combahee Collective is a striking example of how a distinctive black feminism evolved from experiences in the black social movements, the most notable of which was the Civil Rights Movement. See Keeanga-Yamahtta Taylor, ed., *How We Get Free: Black Feminism and the Combahee River Collective* (Chicago: Haymarket Books, 2017).

Robert Cohen, *Freedom's Orator: Mario Savio and the Radical Legacy of the 1960s* (New York: Oxford University Press, 2009); Robert Cohen and Reginald E. Zelnik, eds., *The Free Speech Movement: Reflections on Berkeley in the 1960s* (Berkeley: University of California Press, 2002), 73–102.

For more on campus activism, see Martha Biondi, *The Black Revolution on Campus* (Berkeley: University of California Press, 2012); James P. Marshall, *Student Activism and Civil Rights in Mississippi: Protest Politics and the Struggle for Racial Equality, 1960–1965* (Baton Rouge: Louisiana State University Press, 2013).

For colonial era distinctions between Africans and Native Americans, see Winthrop D. Jordan, *White over Black: American Attitudes toward the Negro, 1550–1812* (Chapel Hill: University of North Carolina Press, 1968), 85–90, 239–51, 475–81.

Red Power: The American Indians' Fight for Freedom, eds. Alvin M. Josephy Jr., Joane Nagel, and Troy Johnson, 2nd ed. (Lincoln: University of Nebraska, 1999).

Neil Foley, *Quest for Equality: The Failed Promise of Black–Brown Solidarity* (Cambridge, MA: Harvard University Press, 2010).

See Michael Dawson, *Behind the Mule: Race and Class in African-American Politics* (Princeton: Princeton University Press, 1994).

For a comprehensive account and astute analysis of the most recent manifestations of such protests, see Barbara Ransby, *Making All Black Lives Matter: Reimagining Freedom in the Twenty-First Century* (Oakland: University of California Press, 2018).

Further reading

Biondi, Martha. *The Black Revolution on Campus*. Berkeley: University of California Press, 2012.

Branch, Taylor. *At Canaan's Edge: America in the King Years, 1965–68*. New York: Simon & Schuster, 2006.

Branch, Taylor. *Parting the Waters: America in the King Years, 1954–63*. New York: Simon & Schuster, 1988.

Branch, Taylor. *A Pillar of Fire: America in the King Years, 1963–65*. New York: Simon & Schuster, 1998.

Brown-Nagin, Tomiko. *Courage to Dissent: Atlanta and the Long History of the Civil Rights Movement*. New York: Oxford University Press, 2011.

Carmichael, Stokely. *Ready for Revolution: The Life and Struggles of Stokely Carmichael (Kwame Ture)*, with Ekwueme Michael Thelwell. New York: Simon & Schuster, 2003.

Carson, Clayborne. *In Struggle: SNCC and the Black Awakening of the 1960s*. Cambridge, MA: Harvard University Press, 1995.

Chafe, William H. *Civilities and Civil Rights: Greensboro, North Carolina, and Black Struggle for Freedom*. New York: Oxford University Press, 1980.

Conley, Dalton. *Being Black, Living in the Red: Race, Wealth, and Social Policy in America*. Berkeley: University of California Press, 1999.

Countryman, Matthew J. *Up South: Civil Rights and Black Power in Philadelphia*. Philadelphia: University of Pennsylvania Press, 2006.

Crawford, Vicki L., Jacqueline Anne Rouse, and Barbara Woods, eds. *Women in the Civil Rights Movement: Trailblazers and*

Torchbearers, 1941–1965. Bloomington: Indiana University Press, 1993.

Daniel, Pete. *Breaking the Land: The Transformation of Cotton, Tobacco, and Rice Cultures since 1880.* Urbana: University of Illinois Press, 1985.

Dittmer, John. *Local People: The Struggle for Civil Rights in Mississippi.* Urbana: University of Illinois Press, 1995.

Franklin, Sekou M. *After the Rebellion: Black Youth, Social Movement Activism, and the Post-Civil Rights Generation.* New York: New York University Press, 2014.

Green, Adam. *Selling the Race: Culture, Community, and Black Chicago, 1940–1955.* Chicago: University of Chicago Press, 2007.

Hamlin, Francoise N. *Crossroads at Clarksdale: The Black Freedom Struggle in the Mississippi Delta after World War II.* Chapel Hill: University of North Carolina Press, 2012.

Heller, Darryl M. "The Poor Man's Carriage: Street Railways and Their Publics in Brooklyn and New York, 1850–1896." PhD diss., University of Chicago, 2012.

Holt, Thomas C. *Children of Fire: A History of African Americans.* New York: Hill & Wang, 2010.

Hosaert, Faith S., Martha Prescod Norman Noonan, Judy Richardson, Betty Garmon Robinson, and Dorothy M. Zellner, eds. *Hands on the Freedom Plow: Personal Accounts by Women in SNCC.* Urbana: University of Illinois Press, 2010.

Jackson, Thomas F. *From Civil Rights to Human Rights: Martin Luther King, Jr., and the Struggle for Economic Justice, Politics, and Culture in Modern America.* Philadelphia: University of Pennsylvania Press, 2007.

Jeffries, Hasan Kwame. *Bloody Lowndes: Civil Rights and Black Power in Alabama's Black Belt.* New York: New York University Press, 2009.

Joseph, Peniel E. *Stokely: A Life.* New York: Basic Civitas, 2014.

Kelley, Blair L. M. *Right to Ride: Streetcar Boycotts and African American Citizenship in the Era of Plessy v. Ferguson.* Chapel Hill: University of North Carolina Press, 2010.

Lewis, John. *Walking with the Wind: A Memoir of the Movement.* New York: Simon & Schuster, 1998.

McKee, Guian. *The Problem of Jobs: Liberalism, Race, and Deindustrialization in Philadelphia.* Chicago: University of Chicago Press, 2008.

McNeil, Genna Rae. *Groundwork: Charles Hamilton Houston and the Struggle for Civil Rights.* Philadelphia: University of Pennsylvania Press, 1983.

Meier, August, and Elliott Rudwick. *CORE: A Study in the Civil Rights Movement, 1942–1968.* New York: Oxford University Press, 1973.

Morris, Aldon D. *The Origins of the Civil Rights Movement: Black Communities Organizing for Change.* New York: Free Press, 1984.

Morris, Aldon D. "A Retrospective on the Civil Rights Movement: Political and Intellectual Landmarks." *Annual Review of Sociology* 25 (1999): 517–39.

Parker, Traci. *Department Stores and the Black Freedom Movement: Workers, Consumers, and Civil Rights from the 1930s to 1980s.* Chapel Hill: University of North Carolina Press, 2019.

Payne, Charles M. *I've Got the Light of Freedom: The Organizing Tradition and the Mississippi Freedom Struggle.* Berkeley: University of California Press, 1995.

Reagon, Bernice Johnson. "Let the Church Sing 'Freedom.'" *Black Music Research Journal* 7 (1987): 105–18.

Street, Joe. *The Culture War in the Civil Rights Movement.* Gainesville: University Press of Florida, 2007.

Sugrue, Thomas J. *Sweet Land of Liberty: The Forgotten Struggle for Civil Rights in the North.* New York: Random House, 2008.

Sullivan, Patricia. *Days of Hope: Race and Democracy in the New Deal Era.* Chapel Hill: University of North Carolina Press, 1996.

Sullivan, Patricia. *Lift Every Voice: The NAACP and the Making of the Civil Rights Movement.* New York: New Press, 2009.

Theoharis, Jeanne F., and Komozi Woodard, eds. *Freedom North: Black Freedom Struggles Outside the South, 1940–1980.* New York: Palgrave Macmillan, 2003.

Thornton, J. Mills. *Dividing Lines: Municipal Politics and the Struggle for Civil Rights in Montgomery, Birmingham, and Selma.* Tuscaloosa: University of Alabama Press, 2002.

Todd-Breland, Elizabeth. *A Political Education: Black Politics and Education Reform in Chicago since the 1960s.* Chapel Hill: University of North Carolina Press, 2018.

Woodruff, Nan Elizabeth. *American Congo: The African American Freedom Struggle in the Delta.* Cambridge, MA: Harvard University Press, 2003.

Index

Notes: Page numbers followed by *f* indicate the presence of figures.

Index

HUMAN RIGHTS
A Very Short Introduction
Andrew Clapham

An appeal to human rights in the face of injustice can be a heartfelt and morally justified demand for some, while for others it remains merely an empty slogan. Taking an international perspective and focusing on highly topical issues such as torture, arbitrary detention, privacy, health and discrimination, this *Very Short Introduction* will help readers to understand for themselves the controversies and complexities behind this vitally relevant issue. Looking at the philosophical justification for rights, the historical origins of human rights and how they are formed in law, Andrew Clapham explains what our human rights actually are, what they might be, and where the human rights movement is heading.

www.oup.com/vsi

RACISM
A Very Short Introduction
Ali Rattansi

From subtle discrimination in everyday life and scandals in politics, to incidents like lynchings in the American South, cultural imperialism, and 'ethnic cleansing', racism exists in many different forms, in almost every facet of society. But what actually is race? How has racism come to be so firmly established? Why do so few people actually admit to being racist? How are race, ethnicity, and xenophobia related? This book reincorporates the latest research to demystify the subject of racism and explore its history, science, and culture. It sheds light not only on how racism has evolved since its earliest beginnings, but will also explore the numerous embodiments of racism, highlighting the paradox of its survival, despite the scientific discrediting of the notion of 'race' with the latest advances in genetics.